I0448115

Insights: America's Voters-At-Large

Barbara Hobbs

iUniverse, Inc.
New York Bloomington

Copyright © 2009 by Barbara Hobbs

All rights reserved. No part of this book may be used or reproduced by any means, graphic, electronic, or mechanical, including photocopying, recording, taping or by any information storage retrieval system without the written permission of the publisher except in the case of brief quotations embodied in critical articles and reviews.

iUniverse books may be ordered through booksellers or by contacting:

iUniverse
1663 Liberty Drive
Bloomington, IN 47403
www.iuniverse.com
1-800-Authors (1-800-288-4677)

Because of the dynamic nature of the Internet, any Web addresses or links contained in this book may have changed since publication and may no longer be valid. The views expressed in this work are solely those of the author and do not necessarily reflect the views of the publisher, and the publisher hereby disclaims any responsibility for them.

ISBN: 978-1-4502-0550-4 (sc)
ISBN: 978-1-4502-0551-1 (ebook)

Printed in the United States of America

iUniverse rev. date: 1 / 14 / 10

Dedication

To the ones in heaven, my heroes,
who always saw the best in me;
Brought out the best in me:

Angeline Hobbs, *mother*
Alma Hobbs Simpson, *sister*

"America found herself facing a choice between adjustment and annihilation; distance shrank as jet planes streaked across continents; faster than the speed of sound; millions of America's people across the nation realized that they had never been so meaningfully; so dangerously close together. It was a time to choose either a mutual understanding or a mutual destruction." –Louis Untermeyer

Contents

Prologue

It was never a dull moment! At times, it was like a roller-coaster ride! Unlike millions of American people had apparently never witnessed before, two optimistic Democratic presidential candidates emerged in the 2008 democratic presidential primaries. People were swept off their feet—in and out of season--for twenty-two months long! "It was not a signaling of **cynicism** in politics. It was pure earnestness in reaching out to rescue the American people from seven years of longsuffering," stated one political analyst.

Other political pundits may have viewed this defining moment in American history as a new era in the nation's political landscape. A phenomenal female presidential candidate cracked the ceiling for women, some political pundits commented; a promising African-American male presidential candidate emerged shocking millions of people from around the globe. Both **formidable** democratic presidential candidates stepped on board the ship—in the raging waters--with answers to toxic lingering problems including social issues--that were slowly but surely chipping away the American Dream--especially for the middle-class and the working-class American people.

For instance, on the one level millions of people are losing their jobs in America; hundreds of thousands of are losing their homes to foreclosures; and gasoline prices are shooting up everyday across America causing some of the American working-class people to be without transportation for work.

On another level for more than forty years, professionals have been seeking peaceful solutions to perplexing situations that swirl around prevalent social issues in a "**pluralistic democracy**," such as our nation. Albeit, to a great extent, the civil rights movement era was a milestone in its efforts to integrate the Deep South with surmountable caveats. Yet, the racial dilemma continues to linger in some parts of the United States today.

Nevertheless thanks to the formidable democratic presidential hopefuls 2008. Millions of American people, especially hundreds of thousands of young adult Americans from different races were apparently so fed up and ready for change, until they looked beyond skin color or gender in electing a new president. News media, on a positive note for a change, gave millions of American people the opportunities to listen to each presidential candidate before making their choices.

In short, examples of some of the social problems in America are pinpointed in the chapter one, *American Dream* and chapter three, *Civil Rights Movement Era: The Impact on America Today?* My comprehensive study contains both empirical data and statistical data, which are drawn on from expert analysts' findings as well as my personal observations. Informal non-scientific surveys are drawn on from the electrifying epic 2008 Presidential Election.

Suffice to say, hats off to the unwavering **conga** line of peacemakers, especially the formidable 2008 Presidential Democratic candidates, who moved with compassion, caution, and great discretion in convincing millions of American people from a variety of ethnic backgrounds that it's *time to change.* It's time to look beyond race. It's time to come together and work together to put America back on track. Rescue the slipping American Dream. Put raw politics aside. Because of the way in which the democratic presidential hopefuls articulated to the middle-class and middle-middle class, they undoubtedly lifted the burdens of millions and convinced them to re-unite as a nation of people. That's not to discredit the efforts of the republican presidential candidates who also demonstrated desires to restore America.

Nevertheless, as President Obama resonated on his victorious President-Elect night: "Tonight we proved once more that the true strength of our nation comes not from the might of our arms or the scale of our wealth, but from the enduring power of our ideals: democracy, liberty, opportunity, and unyielding hope" (*Presidential acceptance speech, Grant Park, Chicago, Illinois,* November 4, 2008). Other American people--especially conservative republicans--remained a bit adamant, at least from what I as well as many other America's-voters-at-large observed.

Since the 2008 presidential campaigns were all the way live, for at least twenty-two months or more, with vigor, electricity, and at times with intense anxieties, humor, and with the season-in and season-out euphoria, my study also includes some startling hilarious anecdotes which depict discourses from voices behind the walls. The characters created here are mostly spunky outspoken senior-citizen voters--*true-to-the-hearts supporters as well as a powerful public influence*-- whose voices were quite effective and euphoric before and after the electrifying epic 2008 Presidential Election.

For instance, some of the seniors had become so overwhelmed by the *euphoric 2008 Presidential Election,* that they brought their children and adult grandchildren to the circle. Some of the elderly led the way to the voting polls on General Election Day, November 4, 2008. That's not to discount the extraordinary hard work of colleges and universities from across the nation who played dynamic roles in also motivating millions of young people, from different ethnic backgrounds, to get out to the polls to vote. Without the influential support of our nation's educational institutions, I doubt it seriously if the epic 2008 Presidential Election would have garnered as many young adult voters. As President Obama, the then presidential candidate, said: "You don't vote for somebody because of what they look like. You vote for what they stand for." (*On Race, Irish Times,* Nov. 4, 2006*).*

Nonetheless, at the same time, millions of American people probably didn't expect the opposite side of the 2008 historic euphoria in America to occur so soon—especially when we as middle-class and working-class taxpayers were being commanded to bailout the greedy callous rich from big time corporations. In the meantime, ironically millions of middle-class and working-class were losing their jobs, health benefits, pensions, etc—while the big-shot **culprits** lay back and took life easy; remained narcissistic for making unscrupulous decisions that severely injured the American taxpayers economically. The culprits obviously enjoyed their mansions, yachts, airplanes and other riches accomplished by **scamming** gullible investors.

But through it all, while the conservative republicans were vehement, millions of other American people-at-large seemed to have looked forward to brighter futures, with the help of the Obama's administration; with the counsel of credible economists who are helping middle-class and working-class taxpayers to cope with **déjà vu,** the soaring recession; and with credible advisors from mainstream media who to this day are offering astounding survival tips.

Lastly, President Obama's performance is graded favorably, after his first 100 days in the oval office. Regrettably, the **fray** between the democrats and republicans continues in Washington, disappointing the America's voters-at-large. At least that's what I think.

CHAPTER ONE

The American Dream

Every day I see less of the country I knew; of the dreams we encouraged under red, white and blue. (Mitch Albom, *Rhymes for Hard Times*)

Overview

Maybe to some people from around the globe it was like craving for some delicious hot apple pie; one that would melt in one's mouth, causing people from around the world to want a slice of the tasty pie. But probably like millions of other Americans, I've always viewed the American Dream as nothing short of fiction. You know like the type of American Dream that we read about in our English literature novels. For instance, we read about the rich and famous who remind us of the culprits on *Wall Street:* lived in mansions, owned yachts, a number cars and airplanes; threw lavish parties once or twice a week with their aristocratic friends—like the character Jay did in *J. Scott Fitzgerald's Great Gatsby.*

But after having listened closely to the electrifying, esoteric, phenomenally political, and informative 2008 presidential campaigns, more people probably viewed the American Dream as a reality—especially when they discovered that it was heading fast down the icy slope like skillful skiers. Millions of people losing homes to foreclosures as unemployment soar.

Fasting forwarding in the following discussions, I attempt to demonstrate the upside and downside of America's *historic wakeup* insofar as achieving or restoring the American Dream is concerned. In the course of doing so, I provide the concept of the American Dream and different takes on the American Dream "slipping through fingers." In addition, arguments are pursued for each of the crucial categories (e.g., education, health care reform, housing, immigration reform, social security, etc.) which are being critically impacted as the American Dream heads down a slippery slope.

Concept of the American Dream

According to research, the American Dream was open to any and everyone who was willing to work hard. In other words, if a person worked hard he or she could eventually obtain the American Dream.

President Obama, matter-of-factly, in his book *The Audacity of Hope* puts it this way: "If you work hard and take responsibility you may obtain a better life." (159)

We all know that the American Dream was primarily made available to all American people, but America for more than a century opened her stellar door to people from other countries--legal migrants who have contributed to the great success of expanding a rich, prosperous nation for many decades (e.g. in technology, infrastructure, medicine, science, etc.)

Having said all of that, I wish to discuss immigration reform—as it relates to building and rebuilding the American Dream. In addition, the argumentative discussions center on other crucial categories such as education, employment, energy, housing, social security, etc., which severely impact the American Dream's drastic "melt down." I will start with education first:

Education. Public education had already been hurting financially in some parts of America for decades. Situations seemed to have worsened during the Iraq war, some democratic and/or independent critics argue. The republicans seem to have different perceptions, according to news reports. They argue that public education in some cities is in jeopardy, but they (referring to the republicans) don't seem to think that spending billions on the Iraq war impacts public education.

Nonetheless, the fact remains. Public education has almost become disastrous in some regions. For instance, in the state of California, the public school system had been grappling for years, trying to resolve the over-crowded classroom dilemma in the inner city. It appeared that things got even worse in the latter part of year 2006, meaning that the high school drop-out rates, crime and racial tension in some of the inner city schools escalated. Sad to say, a web of problems continues to exist in some of the inner city schools, according to reports from both electronic and print media.

For instance, news reports indicated that fights among high school students sometime erupt at several high school campuses where Blacks and Latinos are enrolled. Sadly, some of these fights have resulted in deadly shootings. The reader may find it interesting that tragedies also occur in white schools such as the Columbine massacre, which occurred several years ago. Yet, the white schools, according to statistical reports still have a lesser high-school dropout rate than Blacks and Latinos have. For example, news reports during early year 2009, found that whites have a 25% high school dropout rate, while Blacks' and Latinos' high school dropout rate almost doubles that percentage.

Moving right along, I observe in his book *The Audacity of Hope*, President Obama is made fully aware of the rising tension between Latinos and Blacks that also exists in Chicago, Illinois, which no doubt spreads more toxic on the high school drop-out rates. But I gather that our new president, like law enforcement, school officials and parents, are still searching for solutions to a dilemma that's spreading like an epidemic across the nation and destroying the inner city communities, especially where Blacks and Latinos reside.

Equally propelling, Blacks and Latinos from the inner city schools are lagging behind whites and Asians in education, whereas Whites and Asians are moving far ahead.

For example, in the *LA Times,* August 15, 2008, "Rising Scores May Fail Federal Expectations," the reports state: "By any standard, a yawning achievement gap persists between test scores of white and Asian students and their Latino and African American peers." As he has declared before, a California constituent said that closing the gap is a social, economic and political issue. But he seems hopeful that these complexities will be worked out in the future.

Along these same lines, President Obama in his book *The Audacity of Hope* voices a deep compassionate concern about "black and Latinos languishing in education." However, the President finds that the problems in education do not only exist in the inner city, but they also exist in other communities across America.

Nevertheless, President Obama has made education one of his top priorities on his agenda for reshaping America; restoring the American Dream. During his presidential campaign, he firmly emphasized that instead of spending exorbitant billions of dollars on the Iraq war, billions could be spent to reform America's education system to allow every child—preschool through college--in the country an opportunity to receive a world-class education. However, he warned the parents of these children that they, too, must also step up to the plate and take responsibility. Help the schools help their children. At least that's what I assumed the president meant.

On the contrary, a republican California constituent appeared less optimistic. From her viewpoint, the state of California, for example, should have worked out the problems in public education long before now (i.e., 2008). The latter view point somewhat affirms that the problems in public education didn't just start in the early 2000s. Many of these problems had been in existence for two decades or more.

Also, I observed that on CNN, September 12, 2008, there was a public outcry for state and federal lawmakers to fix broken schools in America. "We can't afford to keep on letting 50% of the Latino and African-American students drop out of high school. There must be something that Congress can do to turn the underachieving schools in America around." To paraphrase, these were the words of a concerned independent news commentator.

In an article in the *LA Times,* September 15, 2008, *Special Program Help 9th-Graders Adjust to High School,* Seetha Metha, journalist, reported on why the drop-out high school rate is skyrocketing and the necessary steps that some educators are taking to resolve the dilemma.

For instance, some critics believe that ninth graders are between childhood and adulthood. That is why the transition of going from middle school to high school becomes so difficult for some younger teens that they drop out of school—some critics believe.

Nevertheless, in the article *Dropout,* in the *Daily Breeze,* May 14, 2008, O'Connell reported that there was a slight decline in the California high school drop-out rates. Yet, the Latino and African-American population still maintain the highest drop-out rates in the California schools.

But educators from the Pasadena School District in Southern California are hopeful, according to news reports. They have opened up special programs to help ninth graders to make a smoother transition to high school. The educators also have parent involvement to help reach goals and objectives.

There are also "glimmers of hope" for some teens from the L.A. Unified School District. For instance, some school districts have opened charter schools, with the objectives to empower students from the inner city to receive a world-class education. For example, the *Daily Breeze* reported on the success of a charter school in the South Bay area of Southern California. Classes are held at a local shopping mall, and students are exposed to intense classroom instruction in the academics as well as in infrastructure and computer technology.

Also in my neighborhood, which is the South Bay area (Southern California), it would be hard to distinguish a charter school from a private school. In comparison to a public school in the inner city, the students wear uniforms. Apparently the classes are quite small, for the school is housed at a small church. In addition, a charter high school has become so successful in another section of the Los Angeles County that it has a waiting list of 400 students.

In short, President Obama has kept his promise in making education one of his top priorities as mentioned earlier. With that being said as part of his Economic Stimulus Plan (ESP), billions were allocated to fix the broken schools in America; promote private charter schools; make better provisions for teachers, classrooms, etc.

Nevertheless, he (referring to President Obama) put his foot down, charging that teachers, parents and school administrators become more accountable for their respective schools.

On the other hand, some of the republican critics continued to be persistent in rejecting the Economic Stimulus Package (ESP), asserting that the plan does nothing to stimulate the economy. I think that critics fail to realize that to make tremendous repairs of broken schools and build private charter schools will require manpower—at least for two or three years. It all depends upon the amount of work that needs to be done. At least I think so. Also more teachers and school administrators will probably be needed; some teachers' and administrators' jobs will be saved.

What's more, I agree with liberals who think that opening up private charter schools in some inner cities is also significant; every child living in America would then have greater opportunities to receive a world-class education. That of itself enables all children from a diverse society to compete in education internationally, as President Obama emphasized in one of his White House Presidential Conferences during the month of March 2009.

Albeit, simultaneously, I think that nonchalant school officials and teachers who are currently dragging their feet in the broken schools--hurting our children--should either be retrained or replaced.

Employment: We all know that the skyrocketing unemployment rate had been the worst in 2008 than it's ever been before; continued going through the roof in 2009. Several news reports—both print and electronic media—indicated that the unemployment rate ballooned to 8.2%; 10.1% in California; by April 17, 2009, the unemployment rate in California had skyrocketed to 11.2%, according to news reports. We are also aware that the former White House administration was blamed for this economic crisis, as it (referring to the former administration) allowed 3.5 million jobs to get shipped overseas over an eight-year period. Worse, the former White House administration did not replace these jobs. In fact, at President Obama's Town Hall meeting via the website in March, 2009, he explained that the jobs that were shipped overseas will not be returning to the USA.

With that being said, I think that it was unfair for federal lawmakers to let the big-time corporations deprive millions of America's workers of their jobs. Not replace them.

What is more, later news reports revealed that close to one million American people lost their jobs in 2008. Applications for unemployment increased to more than 600,000 by year 2009. A report in the *L.A. Times*, Saturday, January 10, 2009, *Job Losses Highest Since 1945*, by Maura Reynolds and Peter Nicholas, indicated that the unemployment rate had jumped to 7.2%; by March 4, 2009, the tragic unemployment rate had leaped to 8.1%. We may recall that expert economists' had made predictions that the unemployment rate would reach eight percent or higher in year 2009. We assume that their predictions were correct.

Nonetheless, President Obama's predictions were **manifesto.** By the first week in March, 2009, about four million people had become unemployed.

However President Obama continued in giving it his all—pushing the Economic Stimulus Package (ESP) that would put some people back to work. More propelling the ESP would serve to save some people's jobs.

To illustrate, once the $787 billion dollars Economic Stimulus Package was passed by Congress, some blue collar workers either returned or were hired to work on bridges, highways, and to perform other construction work. Also, some policemen, firefighters, teachers and nurses were able to keep their jobs as a result of the passage of Obama's Economic Stimulus Package, according to various news reports. More startling, some states received monies from the ESP

to create summer jobs for high-risked youths. For example, the Mayor of the City of Los Angeles had become excited in announcing that numerous jobs had been created for youths from ages fifteen to twenty-four. Thanks to the $11 million dollars received from the ESP, L.A.'s Mayor pronounced!

Nevertheless, it was far from over. Millions of American people were still without work at the end of the first 100 days of President Obama's presidency. America's voters-at-large probably realized that it will take some time for the new president to turn the economy around. As President Obama said in an interview with Jay Leno: "We didn't get into this mess over night; we won't be getting out of it overnight…" What is more in his White House Presidential Conference, Mr. President emphasized that "America's economy downturn is an ocean liner;" there are no quick fixes for the devastating economic problems."

On the flipside, some conservative republicans and conservative news commentators were persistent in arguing that the new leadership in Washington is ineffective; the $787 billion dollars Economic Stimulus package is not doing enough to stimulate more jobs or save job losses; Obama's $3.56 trillion budget for 2010 was pushing the America's economy further in the tank, according media reports.

What's more, some of the moderate republicans and the conservative republican critics argued that President Obama's Economic Stimulus Package and the $3.5 trillion budget meant putting America further into debt. The debt would have to be repaid by our children in later years, news media reported.

Worse a conservative republican went public in seeking to convince the wealthy American people that President Obama's socialistic plan would strip them of their wealth; redistribute it (referring to wealth) to the less fortunate American people.

We all know that the conservative and/or moderate republicans have constitutional rights to their opinions. Yet, they seem to forget that it was not Obama who allowed the big time corporations to pull the plug on millions of middle class and working class American people's jobs, causing them to suffer severe layoffs and cutbacks. Perhaps Albom depicts a clearer picture in his poem *Rhymes for Hard Times:*

> *I see layoffs and cutbacks*
> *No help for the needy*
> *As billions are given*
> *To the powered and greedy....(Albom)*

But to rectify the jobless horrendous fiasco, from what I observed on CNN and MNBC, the Obama's supporters-at-large were in favor of the president's proposal to create at least 3.5 million jobs and/or save thousands of jobs. As already discussed, the proposal came to fruition with the passing of the $787 billion dollars Economic Stimulus Package. Later, Congress passed Obama's $3.5 trillion dollar budget plan for 2012. What more did the American people-at-large expect than for the conservatives' heads to hit the ceilings?

Nevertheless, the economic **slugfest** lingered between the liberals, conservative and/or moderate republicans during the first 100 days of the Obama's era. From what I intuited, some of the moderates and especially the conservatives acted as though they were **apathetic** toward the millions of American people who'd lost their jobs at no faults of their own. The conservatives and some moderate republicans didn't seem to care that the middle-class and the working class had the *economic blues*! I could all but hear the desperate voices of jobless American people crying out *economic blues*:

> *Economic Blues*
> *My job is long gone overseas,*
> *Won't be back to feed mine & me,*
> *Banks closed th doors in my face,*
> *Can't get a loan 'n no pay raise,*
> *Banks 'bout to foreclose on me,*
> *Hear my plea—Washington, D.C.*

Analysis

I didn't realize that moderate republicans or conservative republicans could be somewhat insensitive to the needs of middle-class and working-class American people, until the 2008 presidential race. Besides most moderate republicans **reneged** on their promises to support the Obama's Administration, according media reports. Many of the moderate republicans could be viewed on several cable TV networks declaring that they would help the new president to put America back on track, but obviously they changed their minds. They did not vote to support Obama's Economic Stimulus Package.

Worse none of the republicans voted to support President Obama's $3.56 trillion dollar budget plan for 2010, according to several media reports. Some republicans contended that this plan was the worse that America has ever had in history. This plan will jeopardize "the futures of our children and grandchildren, meaning that the latter would have to be back that the colossal debt."

With that being said, I think that the only course of actions left for the American people-at-large to take is to keep our fingers crossed; hope that at least most of the republicans will have changes of heart; break the gridlock; have mutual respect for all federal lawmakers—whether they are democrats or republicans; work across the aisles with the Obama's administration for the good of the entire nation. Not just for the best interest of a political party; but work for the best interest of the nation. Matter-of-factly, the republican Governor of California pronounced in a town hall meeting in March, 2009, "All the different parties should come together and work together to fix America's economy." A top republican lawmaker from Texas also emphasized that the GOP was spiraling downward. "The republicans need to work with the Obama's administration regardless of whether they disagree with the president," to paraphrase, the Texas lawmaker said.

Energy: I think that we can all witness to the fact the energy crisis in 2008 had been worse than it had ever been in US history. Gasoline prices skyrocketed to $5.00 per gallon in some states. The American people were probably taken aback when they found out from news reports that America was spending $700 billion a year to have oil shipped from overseas. Perhaps that probably explained why millions of American people were feeling painful pinches at the pumps.

But despite all the mudslinging and flickering in Washington between the republicans and democrats, motorists got a sigh of relief. The gasoline prices declined to approximately $2.39 per gallon in some states, according to news reports. But as the Memorial Day weekend was approaching, the gasoline prices began to slightly rise again by at least two cent a day.

Solar Energy. During the first 100 days of the Obama's administration, news media were diligent in introducing solar energy to the nation, which I think was a good thing for protecting our health. From what I observed and perceived, the American people-at-large were more concerned about their basic needs getting met; didn't seem to perceive solar energy as a crisis situation.

Nevertheless, I think that the local, state, and federal lawmakers should not lower their antennas. They should weigh out the concerns about solar energy; make it mandatory to keep the American people well informed about the importance and benefits of solar energy.

Health-Care Crisis: By common knowledge, we all know that we can not even begin to think about enjoying the American Dream if our health is bad and we don't have health insurance. On that note, the 2008 presidential race revealed that 47 million people were without health insurance. Several news reports revealed that some people had died in the waiting rooms, because they could not get immediate medical attention. I'm assuming that they did not have health insurance.

On the flipside, some contributors on CNN voiced that America's health care system had been messing up for twenty years or longer. But the state and federal lawmakers did nothing about it. But to resolve the health-care crisis, the Democratic Presidential Nominee proposed a universal health care plan that would allow all the American people to become insured. On the flipside, the Republican Presidential Nominee proposed to provide a $5,000 tax credit that would enable the American people to purchase their own health care state by state.

Either of the above plans would have probably meant higher taxes for taxpayers, especially for the middle class. At least that's what I perceived. Yet, I agreed with the middle-class voters-at-large who believed that the Democratic Presidential candidate's proposal provided better protection for the American people-at-large, in general, especially protection against life-threatening diseases.

In short at the end of the day, President Obama, in his first riveting Presidential Address, stressed Health Care Reform as one of his top three priorities. All American people would be able to afford health care; Congress would also work to fix Medicare.

Also, by the end of his first 100 days in office, President Obama worked toward keeping his promise. According to the

Wikkipedia, "a bill was signed into law to expand State Children's Health Insurance Program." That was a momentary sigh of relief like candlelight under the oppressive dark clouds.'"

Nevertheless, by May 19, 2009, health-care reform remained a red hot-button issue.

"How to pay for expanding coverage to nearly 50 million uninsured people remained a tough question, notwithstanding the signature health-care issue would be later to debate," according to the *Associated Press*.

Yet, whoever dreamed that the signature health care issue would later become a treacherous gargantuan storm, sending disruptive town hall meetings into tail spins. But the new Commander-in-Chief, with the support of more understanding America's voters-at-large, shoulders it all.

Housing Nightmarish Foreclosures:

> *Every day I see less*
> *Of the country I knew*
> *Under red, white and blue,*
> *Instead I see signs*
> *Of foreclosure and sale*
> *And people afraid....(Mitch Albom)*

Rather than to rehash everything about the disastrous foreclosures of 2008, I'd like to briefly comment that middle-class American people in some states had been struggling with paying their mortgages and home insurance long before year 2000. Like millions of other American voters-at-large, I attribute a lot of these struggles to real estate agencies and **predatory** lending institutions. From what I observed, these schemers took advantage of people who apparently did not know how to interpret everything in fine print. In other words they could sight read everything in fine print—thinking that they were putting all the ducks in the same row. Apparently that was not the case. Unfortunately, many new home buyers ended up losing their homes to foreclosures. Some reports indicated that as of year 2008, close to a million people lost their homes. Had these homebuyers hired real estate lawyers to interpret every thing in fine print for them, they would have not been placed in such embarrassing predicaments.

On the flipside, some moderate republican critics and some conservative republicans did not seem to be as empathetic or understanding as the moderate democrats were toward wary homeowners. Some republicans voiced on cable TV that the home buyers made their own beds hard. They bought something that they could not afford to pay for. Therefore they (referring to the republican critics) argued that such negligent home buyers should not receive any governmental assistance in saving their homes from foreclosures.

More propelling and ironically the federal government mandated that all taxpayers, including middle class and working class, bail out Freddie Mac and Fannie Mae—housing corporations who were in $300 billion dollars worth of debt. This unfortunate mandate was like pouring salt into open wounds. Middle-class and working-class taxpayers were already struggling to make ends meet (e.g., trying to save their homes from foreclosures).

Nevertheless, as middle-class taxpayers, we were being forced to bail out derelict lenders. Added to this, the *Daily Breeze* in an article titled "Candidates Clash on Crisis," 10/8/08, stated: "....Republican McCain called for a sweeping $300 billion program to shield homeowners from foreclosure." According to the above article, the Republican Senator planned to draw on the $700 billion bailout plan for funding the $300 billion program.

Unfortunately, I, like the average person from the middle class, had *no voice* in questioning the presidential debaters directly. Therefore, it had become evidentiary that millions of middle-class voters' hands were tied.

Like cancer does the human body, the foreclosure cancer spread from a serious stage to a critical stage.

Yet, another storm had cropped up. AIG (American International Group) and Wall Street needed the federal government to bail them out of several billion dollars of debt. The federal lawmakers knew nothing better to do than to command that taxpayers take on more burdens for bailing out the golden parachutes, allowing the rich to get richer; the poor to get poorer. Matter-of-factly, in September, 2008, the Bush administration approved a $170 billion dollars bailout for AIG; at the middle-class and working-class taxpayers expense. Perhaps this provides some proof to the old adage which says: "The rich gets richer; the poorer gets poorer." T. Albom epitomized it this way: "....Of foreclosure and sale and people afraid....as billions are given to the powered and greedy...."

But according to news reports, America's voters-at-large lauded President Obama for passing a $75 billion dollars plan--during his first 100 days in the Oval office--that would at least save nine million homeowners from foreclosures. Albeit, critics, on the other hand, asserted that the $75 billon dollar plan was not sufficient to help other homeowners whose homes are threatened by foreclosures.

Another scenario, according to news media, that set the taxpayers off was this: By the time that a solution had been revealed to resolve the foreclosure crisis, the feds commanded that taxpayers' money be used to bail out AIG, a corporation that had received more than $400,000 and spent it on luxuries such as spas, elaborate hotel rooms, banquets, etc. For sure we taxpayers were outraged, but what could we do about it? Nothing--except roll with the punches.

Subsequently, it had become more frustrating for middle-class and working-class people. Matter-of-factly in the *Daily Breeze*, "Bailout Plan Heads for Vote," 9/29/08, Julie Hirschfeld Davis, reported that Congress had come up with a $700 billion plan that "would give the administration broader power to use billions of taxpayer dollars to purchase devalued mortgage-related assets...." Simultaneously the administration claimed that if the Bail-Out Plan was not approved, that of itself could cause America's economy to have a critical train wreck. That type of fear probably gave millions of disgusted taxpayers (including myself) no alternative but to accept the scary predicament from Washington.

A long story short, the House accepted the Senate's decision to pass the Bail-Out Plan (BOP) but with some serious repercussions. Several representatives from both sides of the aisle (meaning Republicans and Democrats) disagreed with the passing of the BOP. Yet, they agreed that "the bill had to pass as the fear mongering was going on, which may cause America's economy to fall flat on its face." But it didn't stop there. The thundering and lightning continued; so did the stormy heavy rainfall.

Unfortunately, the American taxpayers were slapped in the face with another big debt that we ourselves did not create. The Big 3M (automakers such as Chrysler, Ford, and General Motors) cried to Congress to either bail them out of a $25 billion debt or they would have to lay off three million of their workers.

Ironically, the big shots from the Big 3M each showed up in Washington on his private jet. That time around, I have to hand it to the political pundits as well as to the Bush administration for lambasting these big-shot CEOs for showing up in Washington on private jets with their hands out. It was sickening.

I was very much relieved that the Bush administration or the oncoming new administration did not allow the Big 3M CEOs to bully them. Instead, they let these big shots down artistically; gave them the ultimatum. Either they'd (referring to the CEOs) have to come up with a concrete plan or they would not be receiving $25 billion from Washington.

From what I recollect, Congress finally resolved that the Big Three could not afford to file for bankruptcy. There were three million workers' jobs at stake.

A long story short, the Senate Caucus disapproved of a $14 billion bail out for the Big Three. Frankly, after having heard that, my heart went out to the millions of workers who were doomed to lose their jobs, health benefits and 401k's.

Nevertheless, from what I discerned, former president Bush may have shocked many American people—especially since having had such low ratings as commander-in-chief. He demonstrated some mercy for the Big Three; decided to find a way to bail them out anyway. I thought that that was no more than right.

At the same time, I think that the former president should have recommended penalties for the CEOs from the Big 3M. Otherwise, CEOs from other big corporations will get the impression that they, too, can blow billions of dollars in the future; Congress again will no doubt use struggling middle-class taxpayers' dollars to bail them out. My discernment came pretty close to being right, as later in this paper we will see how other negligent big-time corporations came to Congress with their hands out for bail outs.

Moving right along, I probably joined millions of American middle-class taxpayers-at-large who are to this day very much disgusted with these exorbitant bailouts. Yet, by federal law, we're being forced to roll with the punches.

Nevertheless, our (referring to the middle-class taxpayers) storming and raging—like raging waters out at a stormy sea-- apparently didn't move Congress or the cynical big shots from other big-time corporations. There were a number of banks that ran to Congress with hands out--like little defenseless children-- begging for billions of dollars to bail them out of the trenches.

In short Congress bailed out the financial institutions, letting them have billions of dollars at the expenses of taxpayers. Consequently, according to several news media, millions of American taxpayers were becoming more angry and frustrated by the moment. I imagined the middle-class taxpayers, including myself, were disgusted because it appeared that Congress used their power to make us taxpayers rescue the rich—out of no disrespect to federal lawmakers.

Nevertheless by the time that the stormy bank bail outs were rolling over like heavy dark clouds, here comes thundering and lightening that sent millions of taxpayers and members of Congress into higher raging waters. The House had already approved $170 billions of dollars to bail out AIG in September 2008 under the Bush Administration. Low and behold AIG had the gall to ask the federal government for 30 billion dollars more. At the same time, AIG had the audacity to pay seventy or seventy-three of their executives about 165 million dollars in bonuses—of course at the taxpayers' expenses, according to various news reports. Millions of American people, including federal lawmakers' heads were hitting the ceilings; hub caps falling off and reeling—especially when the feds found out that AIG had sent billions of the $170 billion bailout monies to a number of banks overseas.

It was such a big mess until members of Congress demanded that either the people who'd received the bonuses return the millions or they would be taxed 90% for each bonus received.

Even though Congress might not have had the authority to recoup the $165 million dollars paid in AIG bonuses--because of the company's contractual agreements--the fact remains: Middle-class and/or the working-class taxpayers could do little or nothing about the AIG culprits—except pay for their exorbitant bonuses.

"There's nothing hidden under the sun that shall not be revealed." The big bail outs executed by Congress shed some light on the operations of Washington that had probably being going on for years. In so many ways, the 2008 presidential race obviously revealed the truth.

Illegal Immigration Reform: The *U.S. Bureau of Statistics* reports that immigration has been steadily increasing in America for the past decades. However at the turn of the 21st century, America continued to be faced with a dilemma in this regards. Reports indicate that illegal immigrants have been crossing the borders for years, seeking better lives in America—to partake in the American Dream. Whereas many illegal immigrants have contributed greatly to America's economy or the American Dream, others have spoiled it for those with good intentions. According to various news reports some illegal immigrants have resorted to horrific crimes, causing tremendous harm to the law-abiding people in some states.

For instance, in an article in the *LA Times,* August 17, 2008, "Drug War's Costs Borne by Hospitals," a reliable source stated: "There's no doubt that in at least in some of these cases, folks are fleeing Mexico under the safe umbrella of the U.S. But that poses problems we never had to deal before…"

Some of the America's constituents have argued for decades that all illegal immigrants should be deported back to their countries. Other key constituents opposed the recommendation, asserting that illegal immigrants are contributing immensely to America's economy. They argued that losing the hard-working illegal immigrants would not be "a way to go" because they're doing work that American people refuse to do. For example, illegal immigrants don't mind working for low wages in factories and in the fields.

During the 2008 presidential primaries, Democratic Presidential Hopefuls were in favor of twelve million illegal immigrants being granted amnesty, which was a page taken from President Bush's playbook, some political pundits argued. The Republican Presumptive Nominee maintained his stance on securing the borders, first. I'm sure that the American people could understand his viewpoint, in light of the danger that the *L.A. Times* exposed on August 17, 2008, as mentioned above. What is more, a constituent from Houston, Texas, according to an article in the *Houston Chronicle,* was suspicious that terrorists were using the Mexico borders to get into the U.S. In addition, reports from mainstream media indicated that at least 100,000 illegal immigrants are entering the U.S. each year. Some of the illegal immigrants are also using the

Canadian borders. The above reports are scary as one thinks about the catastrophic 9/11 terrorist attack in year 2000.

Nonetheless, the Immigration Reform remained up in the air throughout the presidential campaigns. Advocates for the Reform were arguing that the government should crack down on law enforcement executing raids on jobs where illegal immigrants were hired. At one point in year 2008, as many as 400 or more illegal immigrants were arrested where they were working in factories. Unfortunately, they were deported back to their countries, news media reported.

Yet, the sun is shining in some Latino migrants' backyards. In the *LA Times*, 7/11/08, "Surge in New Latino Citizens," it states that 122,000 Mexicans attained citizenship in 2007, up from 84,000 the previous year, with California and Texas posting the largest gains. At the same time, the number of citizenship applications filed doubled to 1.4 million last year." The article goes on to show that Mexican naturalization in the U.S. increased nearly 50% in 2007 over the previous year, but the national overall number of immigrants are becoming naturalized citizens declined:

People naturalized by year*

Year	Mexicans	All____
2005	77,089	604,280
2006	83,979	702,589
2007	122.258	660,477

People naturalized by state of Residence

Year	California	Texas
2005	170,489	38,553
2006	152,836	37,835
2007	181,684	53,032

Source: Dept. of Homeland Security
Mark Haper *Los Angeles Times*

Anna Gorman, in a *L.A. Times* article, *Too Many Cases, Too Few Judges*, reports that the courts have backlogs of Immigration cases. The number of immigration cases far outweigh the number of judges in the L.A. courts: "The Los Angeles immigration judges heard 27,200 cases last fiscal year, up from about 17,800 in 2000. In the last fiscal year alone, the number of immigration cases rose nearly 40%....Today, 23 judges are assigned to Immigration Court, just two more than year 2000."

Even though the proposal to grant amnesty to the 12 million illegal immigrants was placed on the back burner during the 2008 Presidential General Election, accolades should be given to those for bringing the issue to the forefront and giving it national attention. In the general presidential campaign, the Democratic Presidential Nominee resonated: "illegal immigration should not be inhumane," according to an article in the *LA Times*, July 18, 2008.

Another important point to remember is that concerned citizens at a California town hall meeting--held on March 18, 2009--asked President Obama questions about illegal immigration; apparently what were lawmakers doing to resolve the dilemma. From what I discerned, President Obama plans to maintain his promise in keeping millions of hard-working illegal immigrants in the country who've contributed greatly to keeping the economy afloat. At the same time, Obama plans to work on securing the borders.

Summary

Those of us who've been around the mountain and back more than once can bear testaments that the American Dream has been gliding through fingers for decades. But some argue that economic situations got worse under the former White House administration; others disagree. The concept of the American Dream has always been this: "If you work hard, you will achieve the American Dream." Millions of American people worked hard, but they got their jobs snatched from under them and shipped overseas. Some critics argued that education, energy, and the housing foreclosures were among the top categories that gradually chipped away at the American Dream even before the former White House stewardship went into effect in 2001. However, most political analysts seemed to have agreed that the former White House administration was the final straw for sending America's economy into a tailspin.

IN SUM with the successful passage of *Obama's Economic Stimulus Package* on Friday, February 13, 2009, I joined other optimistic insightful American people-at-large in believing that America is in her very early stages of renewal and recovery. We all understand that there are skeptics who see things through foggy lens, believing that America is on the brink of another depression.

CHAPTER TWO

Awakening Anew, Movers! Shakers! Breakers! Riding out the Recession

"....It is not our character to sit idly by as victims of fate or circumstances, for we are a people of action and innovation, forever pushing the boundaries of what's possible." (Obama); "Recession is a fine time to focus on recovery" (Anonymous motivational speaker).

Overview

In chapter one, the **American Dream** was discussed in terms of education, energy, employment, health care and housing foreclosures. Simply put, these were the most crucial issues that popped up like dark thunderous clouds in the epic 2008 Presidential Election and rolled well over into the first 100 days of the Obama's era. In this chapter, we will observe the actions that America's voters-at-large are taking to cope with the déjà vu-- riding out the recession, which may be illustrated in the following poem called *Déjà vu: Recession:*

> *Déjà vu, I'm not worried about you,*
> *Been around the block more than twice,*
> *Survived you more than thrice, Déjà vu,*
> *Eyes opened wide; defeated you thrice,*
> *Déjà vu, I shall recover from you.*

Taking the Bull by the Horn: Hats off to millions of disappointed or angry middle-class and working-class American people-at-large who figured out ways and means to deal with the nation's déjà vu recession! That was nothing new to those who'd survived the Depression of 1929. The following poem called *Black Friday* may depict the American voters' anger-at-large:

Black Friday: The First One

Dow Jones spiraling down, down,
Jaws dropping down, down,
Fur flying around 'n around 'n around,
People mad--leaving behind ghost towns,
What say you Fat Cats on Wall Street?
Watching struggling taxpayers bail you out...
A mess you made yourselves no doubt
What say you culprits--the least bit?
To struggling taxpayers bailing you out,
I forgive you anyway,
There's a brighter Friday.

--BHobbs

Energy Crisis. Despite the energy crisis that we discussed in chapter one, *American Dream*, apparently some insightful middle-class and working class people beat the overseas oil tycoons at their own games. Some American people, including myself, began boycotting the service stations by cutting back on their weekend travels—mentioned earlier. Many folks started depending on public transportation. As a result, some of the service stations started losing business, according to news reports. The American people-at-large held their noses to the grindstone, according to an article in the *LA Times* on 10/15/08. Despite the fact that gasoline prices had decreased by 30 cent per gallon, many

American consumers kept their wallets zipped up at times. They only purchased gasoline as needed.

In another instance, the American people-at-large also felt the pinch in the grocery stores. Food prices began to inflate during the epic 2008 Presidential Election. As they did with countering skyrocketing gasoline prices, some American people came up with several brilliant ideas. Those who apparently had space available on their personal properties began to plant gardens that grew healthy looking vegetables. Just to see people from different ethnic groups rejoicing and flashing their fresh green, yellow and red vegetables on the TV screen was quite encouraging. It sent out a lightning rod revealing that middle-class people were all in the same boat regardless of race, creed or color. I suppose that gave millions of American people **glimmers of hope** for surviving the treacherous recession. As middle-class and working-class American people, we were at least in positions to hold hands across our nation's troubled waters and lands--enduring the déjà vu.

The Role of News Media: I think that most of us will agree that news media do not have the greatest image in the world. News media is constantly being criticized for blowing everything out of proportion; making mountains out of remote hills.

Nonetheless, I think that during the 2008-2009 déjà vu (recession crises), some of the television networks played major roles in helping consumers to cope with the surprising ongoing cyclonic weather; riding out the recession.

For instance, one TV network, KCAL-9, sponsored a segment called *Money 101*. The expert consumer analyst is always giving helpful tips for consumers' spending. For example, pay off as many credit card debts as possible; do not max out a credit card; beware of credit card scams; etc.

Before and months after the historic euphoria of the dramatic general election 2008, the Suze Orman's Show remains to be very instrumental in offering profound advice for helping consumers to face America's severe economic crunch; the worse since the Depression 1929. For example, people who have already invested into 401K retirement plans should not draw down their money. In so far as buying items such as clothes, furniture, etc., are concerned, consumers should only buy that which they need. Also, to paraphrase, consumers should think on terms of cooking at home instead of going out to dinner frequently.

Some viewers must have taken the financial advisors seriously, for news media occasionally reported that they (referring to some consumers) had become do-it-yourselfers—riding out the recession. They focus more on cooking at home instead of going out to exclusive restaurants for meals.

Also, I think that some of the seniors were quite inspirational during the drastic catastrophic credit crisis. In the eyes of the nation's seniors, the "credit crisis was déjà vu," according to an article in the *Daily Breeze,* 10/16/08, by Melissa Nelson. Nelson found that seniors who've experienced the great depression before knew how to dodge the bullets in America's economic crisis 2008. To paraphrase, a number of seniors drew down their money from the banks and locked it up in their immediate living spaces including the senior centers. I assume that these seniors found safe places in their living quarters to stash money away— stuffing money into their pillow cases or under their mattresses. Apparently their confidence in the banks had dwindled.

I relate quite well to my fellow seniors' courses of actions. Yet, I think that drawing down hundreds of thousands of dollars from the bank and locking it up in personal living quarters can be sad and dangerous. It's sad because some seniors can't trust the banks let alone their own loved ones.

To give an analogy, one senior, age 72, for example, stored $100,000 cash in her safe at home. While she was out of the state on an extended vacation, her niece and her niece's boyfriend broke into her home; ransacked it; found the safe and took off with it. The poor senior was so devastated by this home invasion robbery until she had a stroke and died while she was still on vacation. Apparently, the deceased didn't realize that she would have been far better off had she put her $100,000 cash into a bank that was covered by FDIC (Federal Deposit Insured Company). Had the bank shut down during the economic crunch, the late 72 year-old senior would have been able to recover her money through FDIC.

The above name only a few tips that consumers were offered to help us to remain cool, calm and collected during a nation-wide economic crisis situation, which ultimately developed into millions of taxpayers riding out a treacherous recession like riding out a sneaky storm "with one hand behind the back."

Summary

Unlike it's been in previous years, millions of American people from a variety of ethnicities and social statuses found themselves sailing on the same boat; on the same raging waters, beginning in approximately year 2008. It appeared that the devastating déjà vu economy had affected the middle class and the working class the most. Yet, America's voters-at-large used their sharp insights; exercised their power. The middle class and working class people used their intuition in beating the oil tycoons, grocery stores and retail stores at their own strategies. Millions of taxpayers across the nation received tips from TV talk shows and local TV networks on how to deal with déjà vu (i.e. the economic slowdown); how to ride out the recession. Some of the American taxpayers obviously boycotted some of the service stations and retail stores, for if I may recall some of the retail stores were going out of business; business was beginning to slacken at some service stations. Some of the American people-at-large had apparently zipped up their purses and wallets; spent money only when necessary.

CHAPTER THREE

Civil Rights Movement Era: Impacts on America Today?

Overview

The civil rights movement, which I think was an awesome break-through period, popped upon the radar screen amid the epic Presidential Election 2008. Apparently, some of the surviving former civil rights leaders did not let us African Americans forget from whence we came; how and why the civil rights movement played a major role in the epic 2008 presidential race.

The following discussion demonstrates the essence of the civil rights movement era and how it may have impacted the epic Presidential Election 2008 and how the civil rights movement era may continue to impact America today:

Black People's Pathway to Freedom: The civil rights movement, an astounding new era in America, 1955-1965, was nothing to take lightly. Not even by a long shot. As an African-American political analyst resonated, *it was probably because of the civil rights movement that millions of Black Americans are where they are today—succeeding in life.* In other words, the civil rights movement was the African-Americans' viable vehicle to achieving the American Dream. Millions of American people tend to think without reservations, which I agree.

By way of a historic background sketch, the civil rights movement era was like a ferocious uphill battle fought between two countries. The civil rights battle started in Montgomery, Alabama in 1955. Fearless men and women put their lives on the line to rescue disadvantaged Black Americans from the trenches in the Deep South during the time of segregation. I would say that we as oppressed southern Black Americans were helpless and at a dire disadvantage during the time of segregation, meaning that our hands were tied. We couldn't fend for ourselves. We had no power. We couldn't do anything about our lack of rights to receive an equal education, equal job opportunities, and **equal rights to vote** in the Deep South.

Nevertheless, the civil rights movement era was successful in benefiting **ALL** African Americans nationwide—especially disadvantaged or poverty stricken Blacks from the southern states. I both experienced and observed. Today that beacon of light still shines, despite the racial barriers that many of us as African Americans have to still contend with from time to time.

For example, the *Black in America series* on CNN was astounding in revealing the disparities that some Blacks are still encountering today. For instance, some Black-American children from the inner cities nationwide are still struggling in the area of education. The majority of inner city school African-American children are far behind middle-class and upper- class Whites and Asians in reading and math. It was emphasized. I don't deny that this startling report reveals the truth.

However, I tend to believe that the vast majority of us African Americans who have been around for more than five decades treat these types of challenges as opportunities to grow. We employ the "color-blind approach" in dealing with racial barriers. In other words, we don't always rely on non-Blacks to use the color-blind approach toward us. We're prepared to take the initial step in breaking down racial barriers, for we know where Blacks have been; know that which Black-Americans have experienced and seen. Therefore, if we perceive that our black children and/or grandchildren from the inner city are not receiving an adequate education and that the public school system is at crossroads in trying to resolve the problems with the state and federal lawmakers, as parents or grandparents we take the initiative to help resolve the situations. We come to realize that broken schools in the Black communities could have devastating impacts on our descendants' futures. We take action.

To illustrate, if we see that the hands of our inner city school administration are tied; we can't afford to send our children and/or grandchildren to private schools or charter schools; and if we can't afford to live in upscale suburbs, we use our insights to find another way out. We spend more time with our children and/or grandchildren in our homes as well as in the racially mixed libraries. Besides, occasionally we take our children to racially mixed areas for recreation where they can mingle with children from different cultures. We intuit that in the long run, our African-American children and grandchildren will have to be able to intermix with other cultures in the future to compete in higher education as well as in the area of employment. The younger we prepare them now in multicultural education, the better their (our children/grandchildren) futures will be.

One may wonder why I use the library as a basic viable source to keep up to date with where our children and/or grandchildren are supposed to be in learning. There is a wealth of information over the internet that gives parents or grandparents some sense of direction in keeping up to date with their children's or grandchildren's education should-be progress. In other words, check to make sure that our youngsters are getting what they need from the schools.

Also, the internet may offer parents or guardians tips on how to help their children with their homework or get assistance for them. Besides from what I've perceived, the public libraries of today offer educational programs and educational activities for children. For example, some libraries offer summer reading programs for inner city elementary school children. The libraries

I frequent also offer free literature for parents and/or guardians, which will guide them in assisting their children or grandchildren with homework.   One might pose this question: "What if a parent or a grandparent can not read?"

I've also had training and experience in tutoring adults in reading and writing. So it is an unfortunate reality that some adults can not read due to learning disabilities. In that case, I find that most public schools will have their teachers to work more closely with children whose parents are unfortunately unable to read.   For instance, my friend, Hattie, African American, who is a retired inner city school teacher, talks about the unfortunate situations that she encountered with some parents who could not read.   Initially the parents would become aggressive and offensive, whenever Hattie would try to discuss their children's progress.   Hattie would stress the need for the parents to help their children with their homework. "Some parents would sadly admit that they could not read," Hattie said. Subsequently, Hattie went beyond the full nine yards in giving some of her children patience and help. The students improved in doing their school work and were able to move on.

With that said, some of the panelists from the *Black in America*, CNN series, stressed a strong interest in helping inner city Black-American children who are behind in education, which I think would be a tremendous help for diligent parents, grandparents, and teachers such as Hattie's type. More propelling, an African-American Harvard professor from the *Black in America* series demonstrated his mission in helping disadvantaged Black-American children from the inner city, which is riveting.

Subsequently, I think it would be interesting for me to give a brief comparison and contrast as to what the education for Blacks was like during the time of segregation in the Deep South to what's it like in Black America today. *The reader will discover that because of the civil rights movement, inner city Black-American children of today should have life a whole lot better than we had back then.* Apparently something has gone awry for too long, despite the vigorous efforts of the civil rights movement. As discussed in chapter one,

The American Dream, Black children in L.A.'s inner city schools are 26% below average in reading and math; white children are 67% above average in reading and writing. Currently, reports indicate that the high school drop-out rate of Black children from L.A.'s inner city schools is 50%; the high school drop-out rate for Whites is 25%. On that note, it might become rather easy to compare and contrast the education progress of Blacks in the 1950s and the early 1960s with the progress that African-Americans make today in education:

Education in the 1950s and the Early 1960s: The civil rights movement era was astronomical in paving the way for middle-class and middle-middle southern Black Americans to receive a better education, for I was one of the down-trodden southern Blacks in the devastating mix. During the time of segregation, we as Black-American children from elementary through high school were always issued used textbooks. Equally humiliating, we had *no* access to the white public library in my small hometown in Texas, which made it difficult to expand or explore knowledge. At least that's the way life was in the segregated rural schools in Texas. Perhaps the Black children in the Southern inner city schools may have had life a little better.

I found it very interesting, which didn't surprise me. I interviewed, Hollis, a close friend of mine from Louisiana who graduated from the then Grambling State College in 1960. Hollis witnessed that socioeconomic conditions for Blacks living in Louisiana during the time of segregation were just as bad as they were in Texas.

"We as Black children had to study used textbooks," Hollis said. "We were not allowed to study in the white public library."

Hollis also agrees that the progress of the ***civil rights movement*** was quite instrumental for causing millions of Blacks to prosper today. Why so many young Black children are currently falling behind in education is also beyond Hollis.

Moving right along, in 1968 after integration began to develop in most places of the South, Americans apparently were required by federal law to attend integrated schools. At the same time, the law obviously mandated that segregated schools in the South become integrated. Like many other Southerners, I had pushed the escape button and relocated to California in 1962, before segregation had ended by 1965. But just by interviewing some of the Blacks from my hometown who received first-hand experience in attending an integrated school, I could tell that times had changed by 180 degrees—for the better--in the Deep South by the late 1960s. That itself gave African Americans (including oppressed Blacks) greater chances to receive a better education--out of no disrespect for Black teachers that we had in the segregated black schools. They (referring to black teachers— called Negroes back then) apparently could do no better for us Negro school children than the state or federal government allowed them to do.

Needless to say, the downside to Blacks receiving a better education in the integrated schools is that they faced a terrific wall of opposition.

For example, an African-American Georgian talked about the way in which his White teachers were quite condescending toward Blacks when they first entered the integrated schools. The non-Black teachers underestimated the African-Americans' abilities to learn. African-American men from CNN's *Black in America* added some corroboration to the Georgian's story. The good news is that these Black-American men are making tremendous progress in America today, despite their distasteful experiences received in the integrated Southern schools.

Also, from what I gathered, another downside to integrating schools in the Deep South was that Black teachers were decimated. That particular information was revealed during the Black History month, 2007, on a PBS documentary—if I may recollect correctly. And that particular documentary was true. For instance, my former reputable Black high school teacher from my hometown was reduced to an elementary teacher in the integrated school system. The all-Black schools from my neck of the woods had not only shut down but were literally torn down. My fellow senior citizen, Nellie, a retired public school teacher, said that a similar thing happened in Louisiana. Most of the black teachers lost their jobs when the Louisiana schools had become integrated.

"Black teachers are still being decimated, as far as I am concerned." Nellie opined.

Then I've interviewed a couple of seniors from Mississippi who said that they, too, taught school down South during the time of segregation. But they later relocated to California. Maybe they lost their teaching jobs in Mississippi, also. Who knows?

Nonetheless, the civil rights movement still paid off in the long run for millions of Blacks nationwide. Case in point is this: Black people from my hometown were eventually hired as educators at the integrated high school. Just to show you how drastic the changes were my former late classmate had become the assistant principal at the integrated high school by the late 1990s in the south. The much younger African-American college graduates were also hired at the integrated elementary and high schools in my southern hometown. What's more, by the late 1980s, another one of my former high school classmates from my hometown had become an administrator for the Dallas Independence School District.

The integration of the Southern schools was apparently "a good thing," despite its caveats, for it paved the way for middle-class and middle-middle Black Americans to get into mainstream education and eventually into mainstream employment. That's a hard reality that some Black aristocrats probably don't accept.

For example, they, the Black elitists, may argue that integration and assimilation were enemies to Black Americans. They (referring to the African-American elitists) may also assert that integration and "assimilation hinder Black-Americans from becoming self-reliant." I guess some feel that we as Black Americans should depend on our own capabilities to get ahead; not on those of others.

I agree that I disagree with some of the African-American elitists' viewpoints. Had they suffered from poverty during the time of segregation in the Deep South, perhaps they would understand why oppressed Southern Blacks were overwhelmingly glad to attend integrated schools and become assimilated. The deprived Blacks had no choice but to depend on Whites to help us get ahead at least for the time being until we could go on our own. After all, we had not only been discriminated against by Whites but also by the elite Blacks--most of whom did not lift a finger to get the poor people out of the trenches. But thanks to the *civil rights movement* that gave the disadvantaged Blacks a tremendous breakthrough in the early 1960s!

In another instance, I interviewed two African Americans whose roots are the Deep South. They, too, were adamant in claiming that the integration of schools was the worse thing that could have ever happened for Blacks back in the day. I, of course, held a deep breath—wholeheartedly disagreeing with both of these skeptics.

For example, Joe Peterson, age 60, simply put it this way: "They didn't integrate the black schools in my hometown until 1968," he grumbled. "We hated it (referring to the integration of schools), because the Black teachers from our segregated schools cared about us. We could learn....The southern segregated black schools were a whole lot better than these schools in California," Joe argued.

Thelma Jackson, 66, southern-born Black-American, like Joe doesn't bite her tongue in arguing that the integration of segregated black schools in the Deep South was the worse thing that could have ever happened for African Americans.

I am not remiss, not by a long shot, in disagreeing with both Jackson and Peterson. They remind me of the handful of well-to-do Negroes living in the Deep South back then. Black children from the well-to-do families probably did receive a much better education than us underprivileged black kids. Most of the well-off Blacks were either school teachers, Principals, or funeral directors. Quite naturally they were most likely equipped to provide private tutoring for their children in the homes. On the other hand, the disadvantaged black children did not have such luxury for learning. With that, I think that it is a slap in the face for Black-Americans such as Jackson and Peterson to stone the civil rights leaders for risking their lives to help save lives—especially the poor Blacks. Such bravados (civil rights leaders) made it virtually possible for all poverty stricken black kids to get an equal chance at a much better education; later, an equal opportunity for employment.

Nevertheless, for the most part, prejudice attitudes that had existed from within the African-American race eventually changed somewhat after integration had set-in and the Black Arts Movement had emerged shortly after the *civil rights movement* had ended.

For example, Black Americans, whether high yellow are dark skinned, educated or undereducated, were taught to embrace their black heritage. At the same time keep their heads in the books. Get an education. "Judge all people by the content of their character, not by the content of their skin color." That's almost like suggesting this: use the "color blind approach," even if non-Blacks or uppity African Americans are not using it.

But the good news is that when some Black Americans also used the color-blind approach, they eventually developed strong relationships with non-Blacks; maneuvered their way around the would-be high-polluted Blacks. Using the color-blind approach means looking beyond one's skin color, according to research. Quite frankly, I still see it happening all the time in the neighborhoods, schools, libraries, etc. Black Americans and non-Blacks interconnect most of the time.

However, some African Americans were not in favor of the Black Arts Movement because of critical political issues, which I don't wish to expound on.

In my estimation the opponents of the BAM should not forget that something great emerged from that particular era: Iconic African-American poet laureates, novelists, gifted musicians, Nobel Prize winners, etc.

All of this takes us back to what the CNN contributors said earlier. Racial attitudes changed for the better over a certain period of time, following the passing of the Civil Rights Bill in 1964.

I tend to think that since middle-class and middle-middle class Blacks were able to receive a better education in the integrated schools, more African Americans from the Deep South were equipped to enroll in either integrated junior colleges or integrated four year colleges and universities. No disrespect for the Black teachers from the segregated schools.

Sad to say, during the time of segregation the disadvantaged African-Americans from my hometown were under prepared for college—financially and academically. Many of us who could not afford a college education in the Deep South during the time of segregation managed to push the escape button and migrate up North or back East where a higher education was made affordable to the middle-class as well as the middle-middle class Blacks.

It doesn't go unnoticed. The Black elitists may argue that another downside to integration in the Deep South was that some Southern African Americans attended the integrated colleges and universities once integration had set in, even though there were still several prominent African-American education institutions around. I've met several African-Americans who graduated from racially mixed colleges or universities in Texas, Mississippi and Louisiana. The truth of the matter is that I was too apprehensive to ask them why they didn't attend the reputable Black colleges or universities in the South such as Fisk, Morehouse, Spelman, Howard, Grambling, etc. I feel that asking such questions about a person's education is a bit inappropriate, unless it is being done for investigative purposes.

Nevertheless, over the years I've interviewed African-American parents of high school graduates from California. Some Californian parents are overjoyed and honored to have their sons and/or daughters attending Spelman, Howard, Morehouse, or Fisk.

In fact, in year 2007 a Californian mother was elated to enroll her daughter in Howard. In year 2008, a young Black lady from South L.A., who'd received her MBA from USC, was rejoicing because she had been accepted in the doctoral program at Howard. An African-American father was jubilant because his daughter, a recent high school graduate, was headed for Spelman College. This name only a few Californian parents whose children left the North to attend notable Black-American colleges and/or universities in the South.

The integration of the schools, colleges, and universities all turned out good for the most part, despite the racial barriers in some parts of the nation. According to the *National Statistical Abstract, 2007,* African Americans have made remarkable progress in attending college, since the time of segregation as illustrated below:

The National Bureau of Statistics Abstract, 2007, reports that from 1960 to 2006, African-Americans' enrollments in college and universities increased from 3.1 million to 18.1 million.

Even though the statistics do not give us a break down of the different geographic or regional locations of these particular colleges and universities, one may assume that the civil rights movement played a key role in enabling many more Black Americans to earn college degrees—whether they were rich or poor. I think that this success is unprecedented, considering the fact that there are only 34+ million Blacks in America, according to the *National Bureau of Statistics, 2007.*

However, just because Blacks had received rights to attend the integrated four-year universities, they still faced a wall of opposition—as mentioned earlier. According to research, for example, affirmative action was implemented to give minority students and women the opportunities to enroll in the universities of their choices.

But affirmative action had become a controversial issue: "Proponents of affirmative action generally advocate it either as a means to address past discrimination or to enhance racial, ethnic, gender, or other diversity of some minority groups. They may argue that the end result—a more diversified and representative student body, police force or other group—justifies the means, despite the text of the Equal Protection Clause...." according to research.

Some opponents have argued that affirmative action, like integration and assimilation, was an enemy to the Black-American race. Affirmative action was only intended for the affluent African-American families. "Opponents of racial affirmative action argue that the affirmative program actually benefits middle- and upper-class minorities at the expense of lower class whites." (http://en.wikipedia.org/wiki/Affirmative)

I don't exactly agree with some of these critics. The African Americans whom I know attended UC Berkeley and USC in the early nineties were not from the Top-Ten Black-American families. They graduated from high school with honors and received scholarships. With the assistance of their parents and affirmative action, they were able to graduate from the above prominent universities. In fact, the USC black student graduated with a Ph.D. and later became a professor at the University of Texas; one of the UC Berkeley graduates became a teacher and the other UC Berkeley went off to law school and graduated.

Nevertheless, perhaps some prominent racially mixed four colleges and universities may have turned a blind eye to the victory of the *civil rights movement* and all that it had achieved. That itself may explain why affirmative action had to be implemented in the area of higher education, to ensure that African Americans would have a broader access to the universities of their choices.

Today some of the major universities are still at work in diversifying their respective learning institutions. For example, UCLA (University of California at Los Angeles) is building her cultural diversity momentum, according to news reports. "Over the past five years, the trajectory of change has been made," a high-ranking administrative UCLA source was quoted as saying. "However, more work needs to be done for increasing faculty representation of underrepresented minorities."

Also, according to the *UC Berkeley News*, "the enormous increase in both the number and the cultural diversity of college-age California" is one of the formidable challenges that UC Berkeley faces. (*May 22, 2003*)

Nonetheless, both UC Berkeley and UCLA have faced a cache of challenges, even though "the State of California has a compelling interest in making sure that people from all ethnic backgrounds perceive that access to the universities is possible for talented students staff and faculty from all groups," according to news reports.

However, the wall of opposition was this: Some non minority students protested, alleging that they were being discriminated against. They were getting turned away because of the affirmative rules and regulations. The protesters also claimed that minorities, including Blacks, were getting into certain prominent racially mixed universities, even though their grade point averages were lower than non-Blacks. In fact, information received from the *World Book Encyclopedia* indicates that the universities had to establish new admissions policies to ensure diversity."

Employment Opportunities

I was shocked out of my wits when I visited Dallas, Texas in 1964 and saw such a drastic change in the Texas-American culture. I hopped on the bus and there seated was a city Negro bus driver behind the stirring wheel, something that had never ever happened in the city of Dallas during the time of segregation.

Then after arriving in downtown Dallas, I stepped into H. L. Green and there sat Negroes (Blacks) relaxing and having snacks at the lunch counter. When I left Dallas in 1962, Negroes could shop at H.L. Green, but they could not sit at the lunch counter.

Also, I was amazed when I saw Negroes going in and out of Piccadilly Cafeteria in downtown Dallas. During the time of segregation coloreds could enter through the back door to work in the kitchen at Piccadilly, but they couldn't get served at that particular eatery.

Critics may argue that Negroes (Blacks) getting hired as bus drivers and/or eating at integrated lunch counters and in integrated cafeterias were no big thing. It was only a front just to shut the coloreds up. But integration in Dallas had to start somewhere, whether it was at lunch counters or on the bus. Also, many of us may recall the infamous sit-ins in Montgomery, Alabama and the bus boycott during the awesome *civil rights movement*. At least by the early 1960s, two of the battles that the civil rights movement had fought for had been conquered. Negroes (Blacks) could now feel free to eat at integrated lunch counters and cafeterias in Dallas; coloreds could not only sit at the front of the city buses, but they could also become hired city bus drivers. But it did not stop there.

By the early 1970s, integration had obviously become more widespread in Dallas. Blacks had become bank operation managers and bank tellers. By the late eighties, Blacks were hired in higher banking positions, such as assistant vice presidents.

Even more amazing, black medical doctors were hired at Parkland's Hospital and the Methodist Hospital in Dallas. African American medical professionals were probably hired at other hospitals in Dallas, also.

The above job opportunities name only a few that Blacks received on the heels of the victory of the civil rights' movement. At least that's what I believe.

Housing

Over the years, there have been significant problems in housing, even after integration had been underway for quite sometime. Blacks who could afford the luxuries moved into integrated neighborhoods, but they were severely being harassed by their white neighbors—whether it was up north, back east, or down south.

Nevertheless, I think that the insightful Black Americans who were survivors stuck situations out. Eventually, non-Black neighbors apparently began to grow accustomed to having African-American neighbors. So, the racial tension in integrated neighborhoods is less obvious. At least I think so.

With that said, I wasn't at all surprised when I read a statement made by a USC professor in the *LA Times, Local Suburbs More Diverse,* December 9, 2008: "It's not about color and ethnicity in California anymore. It's about economic upward mobility," the USC professor said.

Politics

During the time of segregation in the south, there were probably few if any Blacks elected to public political office. But that all changed after Black America merged with White America, following the end of the *civil rights movement in 1965,* which was apparently galvanizing.

Take for example in the late 1960s, Tom Bradley was the first Black to ever run for the mayor of the city of Los Angeles. Though he lost the mayoral race by a narrow margin the first time around, in later years Bradley was elected mayor of L.A. and served more than one term.

Also, years after the civil rights movement ended, Black mayors were elected in several Southern states. For example, Dallas, Houston and New Orleans name three of the southern cities where Black mayors were elected in later years.

In addition, research indicates that since the time of Reconstruction, three Black Governors have been elected in the United States.

What's more, according to information received from *Wikipedia,* during the mid-twentieth century, many Blacks have become members of the United States Congress. I think that it is only reasonable to think that the success of the civil rights movement and the passing of the Civil Rights Bill, 1964, contributed greatly to the success of Black-American politicians. Sad to say, for example, during the time of segregation, many of us African-Americans had never heard of a black congressman or a black congresswoman. Neither had we ever heard of a black senator or a black Supreme Court Justice.

In year 2008, the world was probably shocked when the first African American won the democratic presidential primaries, despite the tumultuous challenges. More propelling, the whole wide world will never forget when the ground shook like an 8.1 earthquake on November 4, 2008. The first Black man, Barack Obama, became the first Black president-elect of the United States.

Nonetheless millions of American people won't forget that it was a White Iowa Caucus that gave Barack Obama a big spin-off in 2007.

Equally propelling, many of us won't forget that during his presidential candidacy, President Obama drew millions of Whites to his campaign rallies. From what I observed, it appeared that the Whites far outnumbered Blacks at Obama's campaign rallies for whatever the reason. Besides, I thought that it was great for a number of Whites to become members of Obama's camp. In addition, the number of Whites that accompanied Obama overseas during the general presidential campaign was unprecedented.

All in all, the surviving civil rights leaders were probably happy on November 4, 2008, election night that their grave sacrifices had not gone in vain over a 45 year period.

Sports

From what I've observed over the past 45 years, sports are one of the most obvious areas where professional black athletes have thrived. We as Blacks who've been around the block more than twice can testify that for so many years, we only heard about the only black professional baseball player. I don't recall hearing anything about professional football players neither professional basketball players during the time of segregation in the south.

It appears that despite the occasional racial encounters, many black professional football and basketball players are now over the top. It becomes evidentiary, therefore, that African-American professional athletes are selected based on their performance; not on the color of their skin. Be it as it may, this does not say that the civil rights movement paved the way for professional Black athletes. But I think that it might have had an indirect impact on the progress of young black men in professional sports today.

Voting Rights

Without question, the civil rights movement played a major role in fighting for Blacks equal rights to vote. During the time of segregation, Blacks from the South did not have a right to vote. However, after a long rigorous civil rights movement, the Civil Rights Act of 1964 passed, and Southern Blacks received their voting rights. On the flipside, some politicians give the late President Lyndon Johnson the credit for signing the Civil Rights Bill of 1964.

Nonetheless, the timeless efforts of the civil rights movement paid off overwhelmingly in the long run--even for the epic 2008 Presidential Election. Millions of Blacks had become quite influential in not only electing a Black Democratic Presidential Nominee but also the *44th President of the United States—Barack Hussien Obama.* Statistics indicated that 95 percent of the African-American population voted for President Obama.

Nevertheless, as mentioned earlier, I echo a number of Blacks, who argued throughout the long drawn-out presidential election 2008 that had it not been for the Iowa Caucus who gave President Obama a gigantic spin-off, we as Blacks never would have been able to contribute to his (Obama's) victory.

Summary

Whereas there may be no solid evidence that the civil rights movement and/or the passing of the Civil Rights Bill, 1964 played a major role in the great successes of Black Americans nationwide in all categories, it didn't go unnoticed that millions of Blacks did not start moving up the career ladder and becoming admitted to integrated prestigious colleges or universities until around the 1960s.

Matter-of-factly according to the *National Bureau of Statistics, 2007*, since 1960, Blacks have thrived in education, sports, politics, medicine, etc. Since the civil rights movement started in 1955 and ended in 1965, it appears that it probably had a tremendous impact on the success of Blacks from 1960 to current.

CHAPTER FOUR

The First Family: America's 21st Century Top Role Models

"Whatsoever things are lovely, pure, or of a good report, and excellent, think on these things," Christians are taught to believe.

With that being said from a personal and spiritual point of view, I believe that if the America's voters-at-large can momentarily put raw politics aside, we can perceive the good in perilous times like these. That of itself can help to provide us with glimmers of hope.

For instance, if we can think about the great personae grata of the new 21st Century First Family, we can learn greatly from their tremendous strength of characters that the Obama's have demonstrated throughout the stormy epic Presidential Election 2008 and even to this day. We can cause our own souls to prosper—to cheer up and experience peace in times like these. Develop a strong sense of character, to keep from letting the déjà vu (i.e., the recession) drive us half-crazy.

It was probably just as clear as daylight to millions of perceptive people from around the globe. The Obama's strong sense of characters always stood out overwhelmingly. Regardless of the waves of high muddy currents that continued to rise against the Obama's before and the first 100 days after the epic Presidential Elections 2008, the now Mr. President and America's First Lady stay focused on meeting the needs of millions of wary

American people. The First Family remains to do so without blinking an eye at a mountainous wall of opposition.

For example, President Obama moved quickly to put together a stimulus package, $787 billion dollars, that no doubt pleased the middle-class American people-at-large in the short run, for one million of them had lost their jobs; about one million had lost their homes to foreclosures; and had lost their health benefits plus their retirement earnings, etc.

Whereas these hurting people were no doubt pleased with President Obama's great compassion for them, some moderate and conservative political analysts had a field day lambasting Obama's smart compassionate move. But the Obama's supporters-at-large probably were probably convinced that the muscles of the current President's sense of character had become even stronger after the *Inaugural 2009.* Therefore, they were not worried about the new First Family's,--together with the Obama administration--success in moving the country forward.

Just to demonstrate the magnitude of the America's voters-at-large confidence in President Obama's performance during his first 30 days in office, polls revealed that 73% of the American people were pleased with the new president's performance; 61% of the American people were pleased with Obama's Economic Stimulus Package. On the flipside, polls revealed that a smaller percentage of the America's voters-at-large were not pleased with Obama's performance. Critics argued that Obama was not keeping the promises that he made on the campaign trail.

To illustrate, I was in disbelief about the negative reactions from some of the republican governors and republican mayors toward Obama's Economic Stimulus Package.

Even after President Obama provided strategies and tactics for executing his economic stimulus plan, the conservative republicans continued to stress their dissatisfaction with the Obama's administration.

For instance, I was rather alarmed when I had learned that some members of the Republican Party had organized a Tea

Party--to be held across the nation on April 15, 2009-- to protest against Obama's big tax proposals.

Earlier in the year, the conservatives had organized a CPAC (Conservative Political Action Conference) to protest against President Obama's 3.56 trillion dollar budget plan.

Nevertheless, President Obama demonstrated an even stronger sense of character in spite of the above protests. He remained cool, calm and collective in standing up for that which was right instead of caving to machine-style politics. And even though some political commentators claimed that President Obama came out swinging against the Tea Party organizers, the new Commander-in-Chief never raised his voice; he remained cool as a pickle. He said that which he had to say; presented his agenda with great self-confidence. At the same time, First Lady Michelle Obama maintained her grace and dignity while her husband was getting severely stoned by some republican critics.

Critics may argue that President Obama or First Lady Obama was not experiencing any more back lashes than the former presidents and their first ladies. But one must realize that the Obama's, unlike other presidents and first ladies, had to be super strong to deal with racism that cropped up during the historic Presidential General Election 2008. Some hecklers were making racial-hatred remarks toward the Obama's during the presidential campaigns.

The Obama's continued to demonstrate a strong sense of character in dealing with racism, for even a couple of conservative republicans at the CPAC had the audacity to make subtle racial slurs; showed no remorse.

Yet, through it all, the Obama's took the high road; apparently had too much pride and dignity to lower their dignities to hostile criticism. In fact, the Obama's didn't even bother to argue with these types of critics.

On that note I'd like to interject this: Despite the Obama's strong sense of characters, I think that Washington should hire a public relations czar to intervene between the Democratic Party and Republican Party. After all, America is already confronted with two wars that are destroying innocent lives and draining taxpayers' pockets. The American people don't need or deserve a war going on in Washington between the Democrats and the moderate Republicans, and Conservative Republicans, which tends to damage the image of America. At least I think so.

Nevertheless, the Obama's persistent endurance reminds us all—both young and old--that to reach our destinies, we must be willing to develop our character muscles or faith muscles; be willing to reach out to those in need when necessary; and turn deaf ears to political turmoil.

Further, we may also be reminded of one of President Obama's mantra during the Presidential Election 2008: **YES WE CAN!** That of itself gives us the beacon to hope; to further pronounce, **YES WE WILL!**

Second, another side of President Obama's intelligentsia, per se, probably didn't go unnoticed by millions of people from around the globe. Let's ask ourselves the question: "How many times do we think that African Americans come into contact with Black-White people who are apprehensive about identifying with Black-Americans for whatever the reason?" Having said that, one of the first things that I discerned and appreciated about President Obama's persona grata was that he chose to identify himself as African American, even though his mother was a well-rounded educated White woman who taught her son Barack great values; his father was a highly educated African who also taught his son good values; and generally speaking President Obama himself was raised by a middle-class White family who provided him with a world-class education. At least this is that which the TV documentaries revealed.

Yet, according to TV documentaries, President Obama had struggled with his race identity for quite some time. He eventually overcame his identity struggles just in time, which I think equipped him to become the first Black president of the United States. Perhaps this may explain why our new president is adroit and successful in bringing the different races and nationalities of people together in America—something that's long overdue. In other words even though President Obama is a phenomenally educated man who possesses an over-the-top great strong sense of character, I think that he is overwhelmingly insightful and gifted in connecting with different races of people in America—especially the less fortunate. With that being said, I think that President Obama is willing to also collaborate and/or negotiate with the republicans on Capitol Hill. But they, too, must be willing to put their differences and work with the Obama's administration. On that note, just to remind ourselves of President Obama's exquisite winning communicative skills, he won favor with the prime ministers and the Queen of London during the 2009 London G-20 Summit, according to news reports.

In short, since President Obama has been very successful in overcoming his race identity conflict, according to reliable TV documentaries, I think that his victory could be a great inspiration for biracial people who may be struggling with their race identities. Matter-of-factly if the reader explores Google from the internet and research other academic sources, he or she will find that biracial Americans are having multiple problems with their race identities—especially parents with their biracial children.

Another one of the Obama's personae grata that glows is this: The Obama's are not big heads. They don't let an ivy-league education go to their heads, even though they are both Harvard Law School graduates; lawyers and former university law professors. In fact, during London's G-20 Summit 2009, the classy England women described First Lady Obama as being authentic and down to earth; even the Queen was drawn to First Lady Obama's charisma.

With that being said, the Obama's are well-rounded. They relate and connect with the highest in power such as the prime ministers and the majesty. At the same time, the Obama's use their world-class education to educate/empower middle-class and working-class people regardless of race, creed or color. They, the Obama's, motivate people from different walks of life to achieve the American Dream. Mr. President and First Lady inspire the American people that hope is on the horizon.

To illustrate, I thought that it was tear jerking when First Lady Michelle Obama spoke to a group of young African-American D.C. school children at the White House during Black History Month. The manner in which First Lady Obama related to these students was touching. She created a classroom atmosphere in the White House; expressed the importance of their studying history.

It was also heartwarming to see a group of mostly young White culinary arts students gathered in Michelle Obama's Kitchen in the White House. What's more propelling, First Lady Obama invited the students to send in their resumes' if they were interested in doing their internships at the White House.

In addition, it was heartrending to observe First Lady Obama when she gave a warm embrace and glowing smile to a middle class eighth-grade student, when the President mentioned the young lady's name during his Presidential Address. Unfortunately, the young student was from an inner-city school in South Carolina that was in deplorable conditions. Yet, the young vision-driven thirteen year older had written Mr. President a letter, expressing a desire to become a lawyer or a doctor despite her horrific obstacles.

The morning after the Inaugural 2009 when the Obama's visited integrated classrooms at an elementary school; talked to different little children, I was very much impressed. It was rather unusual for the Obama's to go one-on-one in communicating with these little school children so soon. Perhaps there were other presidents-- together with their America's first ladies—who took out the time to visit integrated elementary schools at the beginning of a new administration. But I don't remember it.

Another characteristic that stands out about the Obama's personae grata is that they are candid but exceedingly diplomatic. For instance, President Obama cautions that he "believes in hope, but hope requires action!" We have to be accountable and responsible for making our own decisions. In other words don't just sit back and rely solely on Congress to be responsible for everything. At the same time, America's First Lady Michelle Obama encourages youngsters in a calm constructive way that they need to receive their education.

IN SUM, I think that the new America's First Family is an amazing epitome and inspiration for the insightful American people-at-large that are determined to put morals and values first; material things and riches, second. In other words, material things and riches do not define ALL American people--the least to say. Neither does money define the Obama's. That's why I think that President Barack Obama and First Lady Michelle Obama are America's new top role models. In fact, a White political correspondent called the Obama's an *Emblem of America!*

CHAPTER FIVE

Housing Dilemma: Seniors vs. Young Tenants

Can't it just irk you when you see young people acting like the devil, tap dancing all over the heads of would-be defenseless senior citizens? But one time, this foolish young married couple barked up the wrong trees when they harassed two timid-looking single senior women.

Here's what happened:

Katie, a devoted landlady for at least four decades, had always kept her apartment complex as meticulous as can be. Every morning she'd have the time of her life, watering the healthy looking grass and gritty walkway. Katie would even do a little gardening, keeping her tenants smiling and happy. Tenants were so proud to be renting from Katie who was obviously having a transcendental experience each morning; in direct connection with nature; squeaking birds from the treetops as the orange rises in the east.

But that all changed when Kate apparently was blindsided by a young married couple who turned out to be wolves dressed up in sheep clothes. The treacherous twosome came on with sheepish looks; humble demeanors; and claimed to have had civil service jobs. Thus, Katie accepted the nuptials as her new tenants. Not realizing that she (Kate) was in for a rude awakening.

One day Katie was knocked over as easy as a feather. Elysha, the young stout cowardice, about 28, tenant went all the way off, yelling and cussing the senior landlady to the top of her voice/1 The young husky female coward cussed poor Katie for everything that she could think of; even talked under poor Katie's clothes. "You need a good (expletive)!" The belligerent Elysha yelled.

"And you (expletive) every thing up around here!" Derek, 30, the pea brain, hollered.

Then Katie went rushing to Edith, in a great alarm! "Oh, that young woman cussed me out and even talked under my clothes!" Katie said in a weary voice. "I've never rented to a young woman shouting such obscenities at me! She even cussed in front of the police! They didn't shut her up!" The elderly landlord didn't know that that same young bully tenant had also tested Edith's waters months earlier, but to no avail. Thus Edith, an extremely insightful senior citizen, from that moment on, stored the bully in her memory bank; kept her guards up.

Edith, an unofficial cheerleader for senior citizens and the city council, survived four decades of a web of bureaucracy; had become a heroine in beating bullies--young and old--at their own games. In her former bureaucratic work place, the culture was forever changing. The middle-age small guy or middle-age small woman had to always maneuver quietly to keep their jobs; cover their own back sides at all times; watch each other's backs at all times; keep their antennas up; not let the right hand know what the left hand was doing, etc. Watch out for supervisors or administrators who might be using young bullies as pawns to harass unwelcome employees; especially those employees who were approaching age 50.

In short, Edith took a step back respectfully, allowing her grieving landlord to vent her alarm. Meantime, Edith was cranking up strategies; connecting all the dots; and waiting for the red alarm like it does on a ship at wartime. Once she (Edith) got the signal from her longtime landlord, Kate, she was good and ready to face-off with the cowardice Elyesha and Derek. In Edith's mind she could take both those bullies down at the same time. She (Edith) moved swiftly like the militia from behind the bush;

quietly and adroitly never looking over her shoulder as the young disrespectful tenants confronted her with blood shot red eyes. The smell of marijuana from their apartment permeated the air. The more the young irate coward tenants yelled lambasting both Edith and Katie, the more Edith did her own thing without raising her hand or raising her voice.

"Edith! Edith! Edith!" Stop it!" Katie whispered loudly, now realizing that she had rented to possible weed smokers. "Don't you say anything to those people (referring to the young married bullies, Derek and Elyesha)!" Edith kept on making her moves in god speed, till she reached her destiny; never raising her hand or saying a word. Suddenly two black and white patrol cars popped out of the blue backing insightful Edy up. Elyesha and Derek began to tremble.

Then after the police set them straight, like sea creatures, both bullies, Elyesha and Derek, retreated to their apartment as the other co-tenants watched in awe, rejoicing under their breaths for Edith and Katie. The concerned long-time tenants were so glad that these two heroines (Edith and Katie) were not afraid of those cowardice young adults who obviously do not respect their elders.

Regrettably, the economic crisis is even pinching the housing market, causing tension to rise among renters. Be it as it may, a landlord should become more thorough in completing background checks on prospective tenants. With unemployment on the rise, people are becoming more identity theft oriented, according to information received from several TV networks. So, it has become no big thing for crooks to use aliases in even renting apartments. At the same time, senior-citizen tenants shouldn't be deprived of their livelihoods and/or feel intimidated at all because of young daredevils who're obviously out to prey on seniors and other innocent victims. But the best course of actions for us senior-citizen tenants to take is to tap into our wealth of wisdom or mother wit just as Edith and Katie did. Don't let young bully tenants intimidate us into relocating to senior citizen homes.

CHAPTER SIX

Seniors Beware: A Hypothetical

Edy, a sixty-six year old divorcee and a professional retiree, had been taught ever since she was a teenager that it is better to be an old man's sweetheart than to be a young man's slave. Besides, upon retirement, Edy attended a senior citizen workshop that forewarned seniors about crooks who prey on both senior citizen men and women, especially relationships.

Edy, at her matured age, turned a deaf ear to these forewarnings and decided that she would prefer to be a young man's sweetheart. Thus, she wore chic youthful clothes and up-to-date bleached hairdos everyday. But Edy was wise, insofar as fashions were concerned. She knew where to draw the line in the sand when it came to choosing young women's outfits. She wouldn't dare wear anything that would make her look like a ridiculous elderly woman.

Hence, the young men in their thirties found her (Edy) to be very charming and attractive. They'd flirt with her practically everywhere she'd go. Edy reciprocated but only with a blush and that was it, until one day she met a cunning young man, Tony, who swept her off her feet.

Long story short, Tony treated Edy like a queen, reminding her of the way in which the young men back in the day adored her. Tony went as far as taking Edy to a romantic dinner out on Hermosa Beach, where young couples wined and dined outside the restaurant under dim lighting. All of a sudden, the light bulb went out in Edy's head, as Tony gently grabbed her aging hand underneath the table.

Then after having steak and lobster dinner and drinking their last glasses of wine, Tony anxiously took the expensive tab. Of course he paid for the dinners out of his Citibank Credit Card.

Afterward, Tony gently took Edy by the hand; they strolled under the silver moon to his luxurious shiny black BMW.

When the odd couple headed down Redondo Beach Blvd., Tony made a sharp right turn on a dark street. Suddenly the light bulb popped on in Edy's head. "Oh----my god!" Edy thought to herself. "What is Tony trying to pull on me?" As slick Tony looked over his right shoulder and stretched his neck to park, Edy quietly unfastened her seatbelt.

Then after parking his flashy roof-top BMW, Tony reached around to give Edy a lingering kiss while at the same time attempting to open her glittery purse. That was the moment that Edy jumped out of the car; made brisk steps down the steep hill, primping her mouth to yell for help had Tony tried to accost her. Her face lit up like a Christmas tree, when she spotted a well-lit service station. Thank goodness! Edy thought to herself. "If I could just make it to the service station, I can call a cab; she had lost her cell phone. I don't care how much it (the cab) costs me! No more Tony's for me!" Edy said to herself.

In another similar case scenario, arrogant Bill, a sixty-seven year old pompous player, went on a hiatus after he discovered that Mildred, his faithful wife of thirty years, was in need of a critical surgery. Pompous Bill decided to chase after much younger women, rather than helping his wife Mildred to plan for a life-threatening situation.

Pompous Bill found a young woman all right. Her name was Myesha, about age 28. Myeasha would hit Bill's wallet so hard on the day he drew his social security check; plus on the day he drew his monthly pension, till he had to borrow a payday loan every month to stay afloat.

Then when narcissistic Bill knew anything, Myeasha had wracked up his credit cards so badly, until his FICO score was going all the way down to 600 or less. Thus, foolish Bill went running back to his wife Mildred, holding his tail between his legs. But Mildred let him stay out there in cold, looking like an old fool. She knew that "there ain't no fool like an old fool."

There may be many crooks who take advantage of dreamy seniors such as Edy's and Bill's types, especially in light of the recession. I think that since some seniors may experience senility sooner than others, it behooves responsible relatives to keep an eye on their aging senior kinfolks; watch out for the kind of new people that come into aging relatives' lives, as some experts suggest—especially in tough economic times like these.

CHAPTER SEVEN

USA: Culture-America

Racism popped upon the radar screen in mid-2009 like a nuclear, especially in the political arena. "It's not all about a Black-America, an Asia-America, a Hispanic-America, etc.! We are the United States of America," a powerful lawmaker resonated. "We are the United States of America!" In a similar fashion, Clarence King, a prominent white scientist from the nineteenth century "envisioned a future when there are no Irish or Germans, Negroes and English but only Americans, belonging to one defined American race." (Sandweiss, p. 153)

Interestingly enough in 2008-2009, some American people went public and voiced their opinions about race, which were favorable and/or unfavorable:

"We need to coalesce….!" a Latina political analyst echoed.

"_____is a bigot and a racist!" a middle-aged White male pronounced aggressively.

Ironically, an African-American news columnist calls a black mogul a bigot and a racist, because the African-American big shot allegedly discriminates against Blacks and Latinos.

But a military young black man chooses to be colorblind: "We as Blacks have been assimilated. We're not Black-America anymore!" The military veteran adamantly voiced. "Military guys like mixing with other cultures anyway….white women treat us better."

"What does that man mean talking about there is no such thing as a Black-America anymore ," a young outspoken intelligent black lady said. "Black-America is our culture!"

"Yeah, well Black America still exists as a culture, but we African-Americans don't have a nice cultural center like other cultures have," a middle-aged native of Mississippi said. "The Japanese have a nice big culture center in Gardena. They have a nice big building. Blacks don't have all of that."

"Yes, I am Japanese-American, because I was born in America," an elderly Japanese gentleman said. "And yes we have had a Japanese Culture Center for years. We have lots of events all the time, and our doors are always opened to the public."

"Blacks in Los Angeles do have a culture center in Leimert Park, located right across the street from Harrison-Ross Mortuary," an elderly Black lady said sympathetically.

"Oh, well, I agree that racism in this country should be addressed," a young Jewish- American former Harvard student said.

As a Black-American woman, except for the name calling ("bigot and racist"), I respect the gut feelings of each race in America. I think that different races of people name their individual ethnic groups for cultural identity purposes. Not for other reasons--hopefully. For instance, some Blacks may call their ethnic group Black-America in honor of their Black heritage. "Let's not forget from whence we came," we as Blacks are occasionally reminded. Chances are Asians and Hispanics probably have similar endeavors. They honor their ethnic heritages, even though research has it they, too, have become assimilated in America.

Nevertheless, I'd be remiss if I didn't acknowledge the fact that different cultures in America seem to be experiencing complexities in coalescing and mutually respecting each other. There could be multiple reasons for the existing racial barriers in America, which definitely should be studied and/or addressed on a proactive level as the young Jewish-American opined earlier on.

Meantime on a reactive level, I think that since *food* is the core of every one's culture, I believe that appreciating each culture-America's food can create a bonding effect.

For instance, when we eat out at nationwide buffets such as Hometown Buffet or Golden Corral, we can observe the atmospheric multicultural effects.

To illustrate, the hot tables are lined with Chinese pork rice, egg foo yon, egg rolls, sweet 'n sour pork, etc., which represents the Asian culture. What's more the hot tables are lined with tacos, enchiladas, tamales, Spanish rice, etc., which represents the Latino culture. And of course we can't help but recognize the American hot foods, all inclusive of soul food, which contain plenty of baked ham, roast beef, grilled hot links, meat loaf, fried chicken, baked chicken, fried fish, baked fish, Salisbury steak, stuffed green peppers, collard greens, pinto beans, steamed white rice, macaroni 'n cheese, bar-b-que beef ribs, cornbread, dinner rolls, etc. All which portray the White and Black-America's cultures' food--more than enough to water one's mouth.

Just to observe people from different cultural backgrounds filling their plates with a variety of cultural foods is interesting and motivating. At least the different races of people are coalescing and mutually respecting momentarily, in friendly multicultural eateries. No frowns; no bickering; and no jaw dropping.

Eating each other's America-culture's foods is obviously not the only solution for breaking down racial barriers in our country, but it can certainly help a thriving multicultural America to factor the equation.

Anecdotes

The Black Votes

"Man, they always talk about Black folks don't vote. Look how many Black folks are standing in this long line this morning. We're making 'em out of a lie!" Jim said to his buddy John.

"Jim you need to make 'em out of a lie everyday!" John teased.

The Bradley Effect

"I wish those ole folks on TV would shut up talking about the *Bradley Effect,*" said John, a seventy-five year old Angelino. A whole lot of Black folks didn't vote for Bradley when he was running for governor of California. Word got around that Bradley used to haul a whole lot of Black men off to jail on weekends when he was the police. Obama has never hauled off any black men to jail. I betcha ALL these Black men standing out here in line will vote for Obama today. Watch what I tell you!" John said.

"John, Barack Obama is a senator. He's not the police," said Jim.

Colorblindness

"Grandpa Jim, you love everybody. You must be colorblind," thirteen year-old Derek said.

"Why, my doctor declares that I have a 20/21 vision," grandpa Jim replied.

Gold Digging: Uncle Henry

"Man this stuff about spreading the wealth didn't just start yesterday. White folks way back then knew how to bury their money way out in the woods to keep from paying taxes. That's what my Uncle Henry used to always say. When he used to work for the rich white Johnson's family, he'd drive them out there in the forest to bury their money. So, when the rich Johnson's died, Uncle Henry and his pastor took some shovels and went digging for that gold that the rich white folks had left for Uncle Henry." John said.

"John, no wonder you lie so much; you got it from your Uncle Henry," Jim replied.

Driver Needed

"Obama said America needs a new driver. Man, I better go down there and renew my driver's license today so I can apply for the job," John said.

"John, remember you flunked the driver's test before because you couldn't see the STOP sign."
Jim replied.

Obama's T-Shirt

"Grandma Janie, why are you wearing an Obama's T-Shirt? You're supposed to vote for Senator McCain." Peter asked his wealthy grandma, a republican, age 86.

"I'm scared of him! They claim he's a real maverick!" Grandma Janie replied.

Politics 101

"I betcha you for this presidential election, all American voters made a grade of 'B' or higher in Politics 101, whether they go to college or not," John said.

"Good for you John. You've just become America's first professor in Politics 101," Jim replied.

A Real Maverick

"My mother always told me that if it walks like a duck; quacks like a duck, it's a duck. If he quacks like a duck, he is a duck. Not a real maverick," John said.

"Good for you John. You just quoted Joe Biden not your mother," Jim replied.

Rear-View Mirror

"Obama said that if we look in our rear view mirrors, we can see Bush and McCain," John said. "So, I went out there, got into my car, drove down the street, looked in my rear view mirror and I didn't see anything but red and blue lights flashing and pulling me over."

"John, that served you right. How in the devil could you expect to see McCain and Bush driving down the streets in South L.A.?" John replied.

"That One"

"Grandma Betsy, why are you wearing two pairs of eyeglasses?" Taylor, grandma's five year old great granddaughter asked. "Baby, grandma has to make sure she sees the man's name who is "That

One" on the ballot." Grandma Betsy responded. "But Grandma Betsy that sounds silly," Taylor replied innocently.

Voting & Religiosity: Deacon John & Sister Sadie

"Deacon John, does your religion believe in voting?" Sister Sadie asked the deacon. "Well, no our religion doesn't believe in voting?" "Why, Deacon John?" Sister Sadie asked in dismay. "My religion believes that the Devil runs the government." "Why, Deacon John, you Looney-Toon!" Sister Sadie quipped. "Your religion is supposed to vote to cast the Devil out of the White House!"

Poetry

America: Politics Centered

Call it like it is
Cause it is what it is--
Need we go to Washington, D.C.
To see birds flying across the sea,
Congress scratching their heads,
Mind boggling to keep ahead,
Of the changing seasons,
Changing for vague reasons,
Seasons refusing to take excuses,
Causing taxpayers bemused,
Among them the innocent ones,
Following behind all along,
Whether in th colleges or schools,
Children learning to obey the rules,
Politics spread to the grocery stores,
Squeezing taxpayers out of every nickel
Like squeezing juice from a pickle,
That's politics awright in the USA,
What can taxpayers say?

Angels Unaware: Navy Seals

Out of the blue, they came from nowhere,
Rescued a captain from a worse nightmare,
Who'd been held captive for five days,
In the midst of the evil tidal sea waves,
Where the sun upon him refused to shine,
Keeping him in the dark 24/7 so very blind.

But little did the capturers know for show,
Angels unaware were cruising so very slow,
Waiting for that very moment for sure,
To rescue the captain who boldly endured,
In the midst of a worse dramatic nightmare,
Angels unaware rescued him from despair.

The Angst : Innate Power for Victory

I can hear it in your voice,
Can see it in your face,
The angst from making wrong choices,
Just remember in th human race,
Each one making unwise choices,
*Provokes **angst** in the human faces,*
Robs himself or/herself of joy,
Blocks th flowing power from within,
Like clotting blood in the veins,
Blind-eyed; can't see thru thick 'n thin,
With everything to lose; nothing to gain.

But know this one thing; bells of joy ring,
If we let th peaceful power flow from within,
The power that saves us from great falls,
As we take control of EVIL tripping us up in sin,
Look in our own mirrors—what do we see?
Friends 'n enemies whom we well know,
And then decide this one thing—lose or win
Either control EVIL disguised like a booweevil
But destined to control us for sho',
Either we choose EVIL or GOOD,
Victory goes to th GOOD 'n th neighborhood.

The Antenna

Walking out the door with an antenna down,
Is like walking on slippery icy cold grounds.
Like a sly fox lying in wait for his next victim--,
Temptation lies in wait for th weak all day long,
Waiting to trip up even those who do no wrong,
No wonder the Good Book has this to say:
Watch as well as pray everyday,
That you enter not into temptation,
It leads the innocent to nagging situations.

Black Friday: Before n after Christmastime

Antennas go all the way up,
Before and after Christmastime,
During the awful historic economy slump,
The worse they say—since Depression 1929,
They fussed standing in long curving lines,
As long as a noisy choo-choo train,
Loud enough to wake up the dead,
With nothing to lose; much less to gain,
To aching hearts—bad news is fed.

Seniors old steered clear of the malls,
Depression 1929—they recalled,
Retail prices dropping lower to zero,
The wise ones still stood tall and taller,
Bracing their emotions in faith & hope,
Not blinking an eye—let alone moping,
Connecting all the dots,
Watching everything go up 'n smoke,
On Black Friday--economy 'n slump,
Wise ones dealt with it for sure,
With made-up minds to endure.

The Breakthrough: Crossing Hands

"The sticks are coming together....,
He's crossed His hands,"
Put His hand upon him n the stormy weather,
Giving His great commands,
Picked up the debris; moved him up,
To th top of th mountain—higher grounds,
While beating Evil down to a pulp,
Causing millions to wonder n frown,
"How in the world did he get th breakthrough?
Aren't many more qualified than him, too?"
"Yes, but God crossed His hands to do,
Chose whom He wanted f'r the breakthrough."

Bright Futures: Déjà vu

I heard the Good Book say,
Amid raging recession days,
"Acknowledge Him always,
He shall direct your path,
I heard the Good Book saith.

One night, I heard the President say:
"There'll be bright futures; sure,
But you must take the right steps...
Amid the deja vu, I'm happy today,
The Good Book affirmed its help.

Burning the Bridge....

Old folks used to warn way back then:
"Never burn the bridge behind you,"
You might need that same bridge,
To carry you 'cross troubled waters,
That bridge that you burnt 'hind you,
Might be closed to the pathway ahead,
The same folks that you step on today,
Tomorrow they'll look the other way,
When they see you walken down the road,
With a hung-down head; holding your tail,
"So, never ever burn the bridge behind,"
Burning the bridge can keep you down.

Curve: Foresights

Trusting n a higher power,
They stay in front of the curve,
Willingly--embracing their nerves,
Like embracing a heart of gold,
That can't be stolen; or sold,
No matter what the bad news brings,
Depressing bells on Wall St. ring,
Like ringing in a funeral procession,
Bringing in the 2009 recession.

Yet, the higher power keeps'em--
In front of the curve,
Willingly, embracing their nerves,
Enhancing their foresights,
Giving them favor good men,
Realizing things won't change overnight,
The deja vu recession n obsession,
Is smacked hard in the face by oversight.

Danger from Doing Nothing

"Nothing from nothing leads to nothing,"
Something from something leads to something,
Why lose everything—chasing nothing?
Chase something that leads to something.

Death Panel: Pulling the Plug on Grandma"

folks, what's
all this talk
about the
"death panel"
n pulling the
plug on Grandma
folks didn't you
know that only
one Man can
pull the plug on
a human's life
n there ain't
sucha thing as a
death panel in
Heaven so cheer
up Grandma
ain't nobody's
going to pull
the plug on
you except the
One who decides
if He wants to
wake you up
or let you sleep on

Distracters: Ways to Escape 'em

Can't it just bug you,
When everything is going A-Okay,
Suddenly out of the blue comes a sting-- to,
Spoil your whole peaceful day,
Distracting you from your dream,
That you work'd hard to achieve,
As hard as the challenges did seem,
Distracters fork up your pathway to receive

Here's what I've learned to do:
Quench the distracters' forky stings,
Keep on pushing through,
For distracters in life are broken rings,
Chopped down to pieces; defeated, too,
Want nothing better to do than bring you down,
Like naySayers always try to do,
Rule of thumb is this; follow your bless,
"Leave distracters on the ground."

Empty Nest

My nest was empty without you,
The void in my life was shallow,
Couldn't see my way through,
The forest and the deep meadow,
Through clouds hovering the sea,
Why did my nest stay so empty?

But when I surrendered all to you,
Bit by bit; piece by piece,
Pieces start sifting-- coming through,
I see you imparting to me peace,
Giving to me Your very best,
Piece by piece, filling my empty nest.

Face-Off

I refuse to
Tango with
you life is
too short
and sweet
so how
much money
will I gain
in a tango
with you
in this crazy
economic
crisis, that's
draining your
pockets, too

Faith

"Faith without works is dead,"
This is what the Good Book said,
So "from the rising of the sun,"
My faith is turned on,
"To the going down,"
Far beyond sundown,
My eyes open to see,
I got the victory,
If I work my faith—
In this ailing economy
Like the Good Book saith.

'fessing Up: Yes I Can

No point in my denying,
No point in my crying,
Load's been too heavy,
Shoulders barely could carry,
Pointed I my fingers at my enemies,
Low 'n behold—I'm final told,
Look 'n the mirror; see your enemies,
Gosh! With these nobody's pleased:
Bitterness, anger, unforgiveness--
Name but a few—from the glacial dew,
Then said I to myself in a heartbeat;
"Get up out of that hot seat,
That scornful seat that's held you back,
Where rainstorms rarely slacken,

Then said I to myself in a heartbeat:
"Yes I can take a stand,
Get out of this hot seat,
That scornful seat that's held me back,
Stop beating the dead horse's back,
Squash anger, & unforgiveness—
Not to mention selfishness,
Yes I can do all things through--
Christ who strengthens me,
My eyes popped wide open to see.

Mr. President 'n First Lady, Two 'n One: 2009 to 2012

Though I'm 65 years young,
Mr. President 'n First Lady,
Two 'n one,
Sings to me a happy song,
Stirring the soul with sweet melody,
Inspiring seniors to pass the torch on,
To the new & next generations—
With Obamas' great inspiration,
Inspiring young people to watch closely,
A new Mr. President n a new First Lady,
Two 'n one with a happy song,
*New America's top role models for **ALL**--*
Rising to every occasion; standing tall,
A beacon beaming-- hovering ov'r a sea of humanity,
Glowing from Mr. President 'n First Lady,
Two 'n one with a happy song,
A historic twosome—
A blessing to even generations to come.

by Barbara Hobbs, Copyright 2009

The Forks 'n the Road; Elephants 'n the Room

Don't know which is worse.
That be like stinging ants—
Forks in the road clinching a curse
Or the elephants in every room,
Hiding the hidden witch's broom,
While the devil disguises as red ants;
Crawling up the legs of black pants,
Trying to destroy both you & me,

Scale back your eyes; then you'll see,
The forks n th' road wearing pants,
The elephant n th room hiding brooms,
As witches rave and rant!
Open up your eyes then you'll see,
Such Evil'll always be around
Until eternity trying to make life gloomy
With tortuous worry; wrinkling frowns?

Friday to Sunday: Victory

*Even though in my life it's a Friday**
In my backyard, the sun refuses to shine
Boisterous thunder is clattering fierce cracking,
Across my eyes blue lightening is a flashing,
Against my window panes, angry rain hits hard--
Twenty-four seven Friday thru Saturday,
Then on Sunday, the sun rises,
Shines against my window panes,
Birds sing from the tree-tops,
With victory my Sunday has arisen!

Future Generations

Though our future may be in their hands,
When we go tired and weary on walking canes,
If we're blessed to live that long,
To watch them prosper and become strong,
Be the best that God created them to be,
Take advantages of great opportunities.
To love and respect,
God, brotherhood, and man,
And shall never forget,
With their God-given gifts and all,
They, too, can stand very tall,
Be great leaders; shall never fall.

Hero

"Better late than never," the old adage says,
From a child up, I believed there was a hero,
Didn't know He lived inside me every day,
Was pulling me through the rain, sleet & snow,
Like an ox pulling a heavy load down a row.
Was deaf and blind; couldn't hear or see,
Didn't know the Hero was living inside me.

No matter what the circumstances say,
Now that I know that I know that I know,
A Hero lives inside to remind me,
I shall the deja vu —come rain or snow
Bad news I see; but don't see,
Bad news I hear; but don't fear,
'Cause I trust the Hero living inside me.

Human Race: Changing Perceptions

Since we breathe the same air,
Share the same economic despair,
Came from the same human race,
With different colors of faces,
We are the same whatever we do,
Whether we're red, white or blue,
I am no better; neither are you,
We're from the same human race,
With different colors of faces.

Identity Theft: Beware

"Everything with a sheepish look is not a sheep,"
Tell me something that I didn't know,
Yet, identity theft is subtle; can make us weep,
If we lower antennas when we meet new friends,
Thinking they're there for us till the end,
But they're there to deceive; plot to do us in,

On us 'tempt to gain the upper hand,
*Making us loose confidence in our **mother land,***
Trying to rob us of our rich African heritage,
If they steal our identity, they gain our merit!
Back to the cotton fields we brownies go;
Bowing and stooping to the in-house foes.

Inauguration Day, 2009: Rainbow America

What a joy was to watch and see!
Millions of people from around the world,
Hovering Capitol Hill n Washington, D.C.,
Millions of men, women, boys, and girls,
Likely fr'm every ethnicity across the land & sea,
Holding hands across troubled waters & land,
Lifted the wool off their twinkling eyes,
Then eyes popped wide open to see,
A brand new era beaming--to big surprises,
Tables turnin'n changin in Washington, D.C.,
Like white smoke, euphoria billows the cold air,
Lifting millions of souls from deep despair,
As the 44th President of the USA--
President Barack Hussein Obama,
First Black president sworn in on that day,
With seamless violence, trouble n drama,
Stirring souls 'n minds on Inauguration Day, 2009.

by Barbara Hobbs
Copyright 2009

ism v. Reality'n Hereafter: Time Out

Don't you think that
It's high time to call
Time out for some 'isms
That erodes good morals 'n values
Like an eroded pipeline
Tail spinning the humane
Society--you know 'isms
Wicked 'isms such as—
separatism, skepticism, sexism,
materialism, superioritism
politicism, radicalicism,
cynicism, dichotomism—
Let's stop to think: If we
Take the sheet off the face
Start a brand new day
Each and every day 'n th USA
Did you not know this one thing?
HEREAFTER is a reality—there
Every soul's from cultural diversity

"Just Older Youth": Deja Vu

Why all the long sagging faces?
The tear-stained grieving eyes,
Seniors in today's recession race,
No need to mourn and cry, cry,
When we turn the young age 65,
Glorify Him far beyond the sky,
Appreciate Him; He keeps us alive,
Stay alert "from the rising of the sun—
'til the going down,"
He gives us older youth perfect oversight,
Beating down recession all around,
On our faces He beams flickers of light,
Alerts seniors to look & feel young;
Twenty-four seven; all the day long

Life: A Long Journey Home

Life is a long journey home,
A pathway lined with trees big 'n green,
Tall-bladed grass along the road with thorns,
Piercing in the sides by evil spirits so mean,

But the sunshine sometimes beams like a beacon,
More often than not,
As the bridges are still weakening,
Life moves right along without a doubt,

Dark clouds still hovering over troubled waters,
The silver lining still showing a heap of mercy,
Moving life right along down the pathway farther,
Bringing peace 'n rest to th' weary hearts 'n souls,
Who stand before the throne every mornin' so bold

"Living in the Ghetto"

Noisy helicopters flying over heads,
Morning, noon and night,
Fear ripples through pillows & beds,
Hope every thing turns out all right.

Noisy sirens go blasting & flashing,
Folks old and young, & toddlers, too,
Ducking for cover amid the bashing,
Finding few places to run & hide, too.

These days good people aren't so amazed,
What were once peaceful places to live,
Out of blue comes the evil a chasing--
Good right out of the neighborhood.

Young people cussing and fighting,
No respect for elders whatsoever,
Got the gall to fight for their kid's rights,
Order to them is a taboo n never.

Love

What makes me do right?
Though I feel like doing wrong,
What makes me escape a fight?
"In my bosom is a happy song,
That the world can not hear,"
What makes me move ahead?
Bravado doubting fear,
As the wicked comes in my stead,
What is it that makes me not gloat?
When my enemies trip up and fall,
Sadly hopping around like scapegoats,
Losing and all,
It's that infinite love—coming from above,
That keeps me on top-- walking n love.

A Caring Mother: Passing on the Legacy

Like a sheep led by the Shepherd,
A caring mother is led by the Spirit,
Listens to echoes of young voices heard,
Weeds out harmful toxics bit by bit,
Like a shepherd, leads her children—
Through green pastures,
Loving her children gives her joy n pleasure.

As she walks through the valley and—
The shadow of death,
A caring mother clings to the Spirit,
Sharing with her children even her breath,
Weeding out deadly toxic bit by bit,
Like passin on food at the supper table,
A mother passes on a legacy—
A legacy so solid & stable.

Rain to Regain

Let it rain, O Lord, let it rain
Orange flames rage like an inferno,
Burning down the tall oak trees,
As white smoke billows the air,
From their homes 1000s flee,
And animals from burning greenery
Amid the déjà vu recession,
The bleakest California deficit,
Amid the devastating drought,
Farmers wring their hands in awe,
Shaking heads n asking the question:
What has California done,
To make her race so hard to run?
What are You trying to tell us?
Time to turn around big time?
Please Suh—eclipse the wrath!
Give California another chance!
Let it rain, O Lord, let it rain!

Living n Dying Alone

Though I'm in the church
Each time the door swings
Open and I lift up my voice
To the high hills where my
Help cometh from and I pay
My tithe and offerings every
Sunday but I turn a blind eye
To the hungry folks sleeping
On the corner and I turn a
Deaf ear to the starving child
Crying from his mama's arms;
Ignore the groans and mourns
Coming from the sick n elderly;
I'm retreated to my own world
Where I can barely hear the
Birds sing; hear the raindrops
Hitting hard against my window
Panes; ah it just gives me great
Joy to hear the clattering loud
Thunder; see the blue lightning
Flash 'ross my eyes as I tuck my
Head under the cover n wake up
My friends and family as thin as
Toilet paper; nobody to call my own;
The hearse carries my lonely body
To the crypt alone; it dawns on me
I've become like Eleanor Rigby

Voice but a Choice

It's like "a no pain; no gain,"
When I don't have a voice,
I have but little or no choice,
That causes me much pain,
Yet, you cause me much gain,
A choice not to dump it ov'r the air,
But go dump it else where,
So I choose to dump it in prayer,
Then justice is done,
Putting your evil choices on th run.

Peace+Wisdom+Understanding=Love

Peace unclogs the mind,
Like unclogging a pipeline,
With an unclogged mind,
Wisdom flows through to—
Till it reaches Understanding,
Like water flowing thru,
An unclogged pipeline,
To the main line in demand,

Put them all three together,
In the midst of stormy weather:
Peace+Wisdom+Understanding,
Operative n a clear mind; n time,
At the end of the day—
Love is in greatest command.

Power Play: "A Race against Time"

Dear Friends of the Day:

I have not time for power play,
Life is too short and sweet,
Doctors can't hear my every heart beat.
Power play separates the best of friends,
Soon comes to an end,
Someone with true power stepped in.

I know who I am—where I'm going,
Refuse to carry power play along,
Power players ultimately lose; look bad,
Even their faces look sad,
Lose the dearest friendships they ever had,
So you see why I have no time for strife,
Choose to move on—enjoy the good life.

Mr. President 'n First Lady, Two 'n One: 2009 to 2012

Though I'm 65 years young,
Mr. President 'n First Lady,
Two 'n one,
Sings to me a happy song,
Stirring the soul with sweet melody,
Inspiring seniors to pass the torch on,
To the new & next generations—
With Obamas' great inspiration,
Inspiring young people to watch closely,
A new Mr. President n a new First Lady,
Two 'n one with a happy song,
*New America's top role models for **ALL**--*
Rising to every occasion; standing tall,
A beacon beaming-- hovering ov'r a sea of humanity,
Glowing from Mr. President 'n First Lady,
Two 'n one with a happy song
A historic twosome--
A blessing to even generations to come.

Preventable Disease

When you n yours inflict evil wounds
Like stinging vicious mosquitoes,
I move quickly to forgive you both,
So your inflicted evil wounds,
Won't infect my mind, body n soul.
I move quickly to forgive you both,
To keep the anointing flowing,
Through my mind, body, and soul,
Flowing like running living waters,
Washing away your inflicted wounds.

Radar Screen

You keep th radar on all th time,
Trying to destroy human minds,
Like a GPS tracking every mile,
You track to make people frown,
Trying to keep'em from smiling,
But little do you know for sho,'
I be keeping the radar on you 24/7,
Day in day out even in the snow,
As wisdom beamin' from heaven,
Guides n shows me just what to do,
To blindside your evil radar, too,
At the end of the day, you're thru.

Retirees: Today vs. Yesterday

Retirement ain't like it used to be,
Where you'd flop on th' big rockin' chair,
On the serene veranda; under healthy shade trees,
Mockingbirds sing as you breathe clean fresh air,
Or go cruising the peaceful Atlantic Ocean,
Relaxing on the peaceful cruise ship,
Enjoying your retirement portions,
As the quiet blue waters the whales whip.

Retirement today sings a different song,
Keeps the minds 'n bodies sharp 'n strong,
Keeps unplugged ears to hear,
Scam artists seekin' to prey on seniors,
Like the worse kind of fender benders,
Over the telephones—at the peaceful homes,
At ATMs in the A.M.; 'n the P.M.
Retirement ain't like it used to be,
Eyes 'n minds are open wide to see.

Road to Nowhere

When I first met you, I carried a heavy load
Shoulders weakening every second
You came along and shared my load
Big sigh of relief was my innocent belief
Thought I could depend on you to see me through
To the end of the icy road; help me to unload

Next thing I knew midway the icy road
You'd dumped your load on my load
Weighed me down with tiers; for generation years
When I came closer to Him somewhere up there,
He picked up my heavy load; from the icy road,
The load you left for me was a road to nowhere

Roots 'n Human Race

Some may trace my roots to Africa,
Others may trace my roots to Ireland,
Some even may trace my roots to India,
But no matter what the historians say,
This one thing for sure I know,
All roots are traced to th Garden of Eden,
The whole human race started there for sho.'

By Barbara Hobbs
Copyright 2009

Shadows: Building a Legacy

Step by step somebody's in my shadow,
Watching every move I make,
As the deja vu echoes thru the meadows,
They watch which road I take,
North, East, West or South,
They watch the choices I make,
Keeping closed their mouths,
Then I come to realize one thing:
"Brick by brick" keep building a legacy,
One that'll make 'em with joy sing,
My descendants depend on me,
To leave behind a good solid legacy.

Skepticism: What Say You Young Lad?

No wonder Sistuh Brooks once said:
"You be cool; you be real cool,"
I reckon her advice following my bliss,
That goes something this:
"When you be cool; be real cool;
Somebody shows up in y'r sted,
Then you put y'r foot on the stool,
Watch 'em make hard their beds,
Then you're become to reason this:
"Since skeptics didn't make me",
Skeptics can't mold me,
Since skeptics didn't shape me,
Then Skeptics can't break me,"
Your skeptics, young lad: what say you?

Time

Time is like a season,
Changes for a reason,
Catches us by surprise,
Never answers the question, why?
Fearlessly moves right along,
Like the nonchalant soul in bold,
Hearing no evil, seeing no evil,
Like a nonchalant Bo weevil,
Chippin away at soon-to-be bygones,
It leaves behind yesteryear,
Changes with no fear,
It's colorless, odorless, tasteless,
Time is motionless,
Time is like a season,
Time changes for a reason.

The Universe: Everyman; Everywoman

Like Mother Nature takes control
Everyman; everywoman can take
Control his or her universe
Like Mother Nature decides--
To let it storm all day 'n out
Let it storm throughout the night
Then lets the sun shine bright
Brightening up the whole day
Then lets the moon & the stars
Lighten up the skies for a while--
The skies at night so very bright
Mother Nature controls all right--
Her own universe.

Like Mother Nature, I surmise--
Everyman; everywoman can gain
Control of his or her own universe
Everyman; everywoman can make
His or her life better or worse;
For everyman; everywoman can
With His wisdom guide--
Can take control of his or her life
Swallowing up the poisonous pride
Shunning the toxic strife
Everyman; every woman makes life better--
Or makes life worse for his or her universe.

Young People: Facing Reality

Young people, there's nothing like facing reality,
Nothing worse than wallowing in self-pity,
For self-pity is like a treacherous hawk in the air,
Flying low 'n hunting looking for souls to snare,
Knows fully well self-pity is getting 'em nowhere,
Take it from me, walked in y'r shoes a plenty days,
Wallowing in self-pity drowned me in every way.
No wonder I'm revived to tell you a thing or two,
Self-pity is your own worse enemy, too.
But facing reality defeats that enemy--self-pity,
Facing reality opens th door to great opportunities
Opens up the mind wide to perceive the enemies.

Epilogue

Together we stand; divided we shall fall. It was astounding that more than fifty million American voters used their sharp insights to put aside their differences and elect a president who's people-oriented; a commander-in-chief who connects with people from different races and different nationalities around the globe; whether they are rich, middle-class or middle-middle class; or whether they are young or old.

Politely put, in a likewise fashion, hopefully the Democrats and Republicans on Capitol Hill will reconcile and ban together; put their differences on hold and start focusing more on resolving the urgent issues that our nation is facing today: an ailing economy, which is all inclusive of a high unemployment rate, the highest in some regions such as southern California since the *Depression 1929*; big bailouts, more than a trillion-dollar deficit, energy, healthcare, housing, education, the exorbitant costs of the Iraq and the Afghanistan wars and a gamut of other issues.

Critics from the right may argue that it is the president's job to bring the Democrats and Republicans together in Washington. Apparently, that's easier said than done. That is why I think that Washington should hire a disinterested public relations czar to mediate between the two political parties on Capitol Hill.

A prominent California judge put it this way: "Times are changing around the globe; we also have to change."

Despite the overloaded plate that the new president inherited and carries, the polls showed that President Obama received an approval rating of 68% for his **first 100 days'** performance; 32% disapproval rating. But the drama continues, as insightful America's-voters-at-large are picking up the pieces and moving on with their lives. At least from what I observe.

Bibliography

What Should be Taxed to Pay for Health Care?, May 19, 2009. *Associated Press.*

Black in America, Series, CNN, 2008.

Daily Breeze, Sept. 29, 2008, *Bailout Plan Heads for Vote,* Julie Hirschfeld-Davis.

KCAL 9 News, Money 101.

KCET, www.coldblind.com 2008.

Los Angeles Times, Jan. 10, 2008, The Worse Since 1945.... Reynolds and Nicholas.

Los Angeles Times, July 11, 2008. *Surge in New Latino Citizens.*

Los Angeles Times, Aug. 2, 2008. *Unemployment at Highest in Four Years*

Los Angeles Times, Aug. 15, 2008, *Rising Scores May Fail Federal Expectations; Program Helps Graders Adjust to High School.* Seetha Metha.

Los Angeles Times, Feb. 3, 2009, *GOP Set into Carve Stimulus.* Janet Hook and Maura Reynolds.

National Statistical Abstract, 2007.

Obama, Barack (44th President of the United States), The Audacity of Hope.

Press-Telegram, March 21, 2009, *Seal Beach's Naval Station to Get $7.7M.*

Rogak, Lisa, Obama Barack in His own Words: Presidential Acceptance Speech, Grant Park,
Chicago, Illinois, November 4, 2008.
Rogak, Lisa, Obama Barack in His own Words: "Cutting Cost and Covering America:..."
May 29, 2007.
Sandweiss, Martha, "Crossing Strange," 2009, p. 153
UC Berkeley News, May 22, 2003.
Wikipedia (http://en.wikipedia.olrg/wiki/) Affirmative Action.

Glossary

callous	hardened; thickened; heartless; insensitive; etc.
culprit	The person guilty of an offense or misdeed.
cynicism	An attitude of scornful or jaded negativity, especially a general distrust of the integrity or professed motives of others.
déjà vu	Déjà vu or promesia, is the experience of feeling sure that one has witnessed or experienced a new situation previously, although the exact circumstances of the previous encounter are uncertain.
epic	An epic is a lengthy narrative poem, ordinarily concerning a Serious subject containing details of heroic deeds and events significant to a nation.
glimmers of hope	Twinkles of light shining on a dreary situations.
power play	A power play, as per Claude Steiner, [1] (http:// www. Claudesteiner.com) is an interpersonal transaction or maneuver in which one person attempts to control another against his or her will.
predatory lenders	Taking advantage of innocent investors who don't read or interpret everything in fine print.
renege	go back on; break your word; break a promise; etc

ricocheted	recoil; reverberate; rebound; echo; glance off, etc.
scam	fraud; dishonesty; cheating; etc.
skepticism	cynicism; disbelief; doubt; uncertainty; etc.
vigor	energy; dynamism; drive; vitality; verve; gusto; etc.

Appendix

People naturalized by year*

Year	Mexicans	All____
2005	77,089	604,280
2006	83,979	702,589
2007	122.258	660,477

People naturalized by state of Residence

Year	California	Texas
2005	170,489	38,553
2006	152,836	37,835
2007	181,684	53,032

Source: Dept. of Homeland Security
Mark Haper *Los Angeles Times*

Acknowledgements

I am grateful for so many wonderful people. But first and foremost, I wish to express my thanks to Father God who gave me the courage to step out on faith and have the guts to write and publish my first comprehensive American story that covers an electrifying epic Presidential Election such as the 2008 presidential race; the **first 100 days** of a new president's era, and an American comprehensive story that observes the sharp insights of my fellow American citizens-at-large.

With further due respect, I thank the professionals from the Inglewood City Library and the Los Angeles County Library who took out the time from their busy schedules to answer many complex questions that may have, otherwise, seemed silly to some other patrons.

I do not hesitate to acknowledge my only offspring, chief medical corpsman Dexter Hall, also a grad student and an avid reader, who's always been my right arm and gutsy critic of my published works ever since his high school days. Neither will I ever forget some of the good people from Los Angeles Community College District, former place of employment, who always encouraged me to write and publish my works.

Also, I wish to thank my fellow retired senior citizens and some young adults from various ethnicities who shared their true-to-the heart gut feelings throughout the electrifying epic 2008 Presidential Election and many days after President Obama was sworn into office.

About the Author

Barbara Hobbs holds a Bachelor's of Arts degree in public relations and a graduate program Certificate of Completion in Rhetoric and Composition from California State University at Dominguez Hills. In addition, she holds an associate in arts degree in business education from Los Angeles Metropolitan College (now L. A. Trade-Technical College); and a Teaching Certificate from the University of California. Barbara Hobbs is a retired community relations employee from the Los Angeles Community Colleges where she worked for thirty-seven long years; worked in corporate America for four years in the early 1960s. Upon retirement, Hobbs served as a volunteer reading-by-9 tutor for the Los Angeles Unified School District. Barbara later joined the Book Club at A.C. Bilbrew Library of the Los Angeles County. She's been an avid reader and a prolific writer ever since age nine; became a Sunday school secretary at age 12, following in the footsteps of her oldest late sister and mentor, Alma.

Barbara Hobbs' literary achievements include her self-published book of poetry, in 1996, entitled *Conquering Obstacles*. In 2008, Hobbs parachuted her unfailing faith and published her first book of short stories and universal poems called *Black America, 1956-1966: The Break-Through Period*. Brick by brick, she built up "the audacity of hope;" became brave enough to write and publish her first American story, *Insights: America's Voters-At-Large*. Barbara Hobbs had the honor of receiving a "thank you letter" from President Obama for two poems that she wrote and forwarded to the Obama's entitled: *Inauguration 2009: Rainbow America* and *Mr. President 'n First Lady: 2009-2012*.

Born in Texas, Barbara Hobbs is the proud mother of one son, USCG Chief Petty Officer Dexter Hall; a proud grandmother of one grandchild, Gabrielle Adoniah Hall, age 7.

www.ingramcontent.com/pod-product-compliance
Lightning Source LLC
Chambersburg PA
CBHW051412280526
45785CB00003B/1045